PRAISE FOR *FROM CONFLICT TO CREATIVE COLLABORATION*

Creativity is real ... and it can be awakened to spark breakthroughs in situations that otherwise seem hopeless. I have dedicated my life to learning how to release this potential in people.

Rosa Zubizarreta has a similar passion, showing an immediate love for Dynamic Facilitation from the moment she experienced it. I'm really happy to recommend this clear and helpful guide to make the practice more accessible to all of us... so we can spark breakthrough progress on today's biggest problems.

Jim Rough, originator of Dynamic Facilitation, founder of Dynamic Facilitation Associates

I am deeply grateful to Rosa Zubizarreta for writing this excellent book on a pathbreaking method for working with groups. I have been practicing and teaching Dynamic Facilitation for over five years in the German-speaking part of Europe. An astonishing number of participants who attend our seminars write us enthusiastic e-mails afterward, describing what they have achieved by applying Dynamic Facilitation in very difficult situations. They are delighted about the breakthroughs they have been able to facilitate.

Matthias zur Bonsen, author, organizational consultant, and trainer
http://www.leading-with-life.de

D0839700

As our world becomes more complex and challenging, there is a crucial need for creative collaboration. Dynamic Facilitation is a breakthrough innovation for guiding groups through the hard work of solving shared problems and creating new possibilities. In this book, Rosa Zubizarreta provides a detailed, practical, and effective guide for facilitating a group's progress toward significant breakthrough thinking, planning, and action.

> Saul Eisen, Ph.D.
> Principal, Human Systems Development; Author of *Nine Assumptions and Ten Realities;* Founder Emeritus of the Organization Development program at Sonoma State University

Rosa is a gifted facilitator: she listens with exquisite sensitivity, creates a safe space for open expression of different points of view, and is adept at gently navigating conflict in a group so that all parties feel valued and respected for their contributions. She does all this with warmth and a genuinely engaging sense of humor. I highly recommend her work, as well as this book she has written to share her knowledge with others.

> Anne Grosser
> Imago Therapist and Co-founder of the Center for Compassionate Relationships

Dynamic Facilitation helps people feel heard and let go of their pre-set thinking and their attachments. This allows highly creative solutions to emerge. It all happens in a non-linear way; the results are obvious afterwards, yet not foreseeable during the process. I think this approach to real choice-creating is the next big thing we need to learn for the well-being of our organizations and of society. DF is just the beginning!

> Holger Scholz, founder of Kommunikationslotsen, IAF Certified Facilitator, and Facilitation Trainer

FROM
CONFLICT
TO
CREATIVE
COLLABORATION

FROM
CONFLICT
TO
CREATIVE
COLLABORATION

A User's Guide to Dynamic Facilitation

ROSA ZUBIZARRETA

TWOHARBORS
WWW.TWOHARBORSPRESS.COM

Two Harbors Press
322 First Avenue N, 5th Floor
Minneapolis, MN 55401
612.455.2293
www.TwoHarborsPress.com

ISBN-13: 978-1-62652-611-2
LCCN: 2014900061

Distributed by Itasca Books

Cover Design by Steve Porter
Typeset by Kristeen Ott

Illustrations by Nancy Margulis, used with permission.

Front cover photos: Top left, Dynamic Facilitation Associates. Used with permission. Top right, bottom right, and bottom left: Energieinstitute and Büro für Zukunftsfragen, Vorarlberg, Austria. Used with permission.

Back cover photo by Elmar Kruithoff, used with permission.

Printed in the United States of America

To the memory of Ted Heinz,
an enthusiastic visionary and dedicated supporter of this work.

CONTENTS

THE TRANSFORMATIVE POWER OF REFLECTION

Like many good things, I learned about Dynamic Facilitation (DF) and Rosa Zubizarreta through a friend. I met Tom Atlee because of a book I co-edited, *The Change Handbook*. It is a collection of system-wide change practices, and the first edition didn't include DF. Tom was adamant that I learn about the process. Both Tom and I are long-time students of conversational practices that enable diverse, even conflicted groups to engage and reach useful outcomes. He insisted that Dynamic Facilitation was unique and that any compilation needed to include it. It took him a while to convince me, but I finally attended a workshop conducted by DF creator Jim Rough. Tom was right. DF brings some distinctive gifts to the mix of engagement practices. And Rosa contributed to Jim's great creation by articulating a principle-based foundation. Her first version of the user's guide that you now hold helped me to make sense of the process.

What attracts me most about DF is the transformative power of reflection that I experience at its heart. During that first workshop, I watched others and experienced myself changing as we each responded to the simple act of having our words and feeling played back to us. I discovered more compassion and tolerance for another's perspective as their story emerged. I became better equipped to tackle a challenging issue because I could relate to their humanity even when we held different opinions about a subject.

Useful for any complex situation, when conflict runs hot or bad blood exists, DF thrives. It succeeds by welcoming whatever shows up. It uses the insight of aikido, harnessing the other's energy and reflecting it back to the group. And that elicits authentic, heartfelt expressions from participants. DF brilliantly engages us in the art of reflection, of listening deeply, of witnessing each other. The Dynamic Facilitator acts as a mirror—repeating our words or describing our feelings. She helps us to hear each other and ourselves. She supports us in stepping into the fire of our passionately held beliefs and noticing larger possibilities taking shape among us. In doing so, DF helps us to get underneath ineffective expressions—shouting, whining, bullying—to the deeper longings buried in the angst. It clarifies the heart of our cries. Perhaps it helps someone to realize what they want to express for the first time. Feeling fully heard frees us to listen to others, to notice our differences and yet stay connected. Through that process, shared meaning coalesces. We discover a larger, more complex picture painted by our diverse views. That bigger picture is often an unexpected, coherent response that could not have arisen without deep expressions at the heart of our differences.

The remarkable result of Dynamic Facilitation: it consistently helps groups to arrive at broadly shared outcomes. No matter how conflicted, by taking participants deeply into what matters to them, this practice turns conflict into inspiration. Breakthrough solutions arise that draw from what is most essential to everyone involved. The process can be so gradual that only after the fact do the elegantly simple solutions that consistently surface seem revolutionary.

A skilled Dynamic Facilitator makes the process appear deceptively easy. It looks like she is simply calling on people and writing down what they say. Yet participants come away changed, with solutions that everyone likes. As with any good support service—room lighting, garbage pickup, electrical power—we only notice when it's not working. Otherwise, the process and the intense work done by the facilitator are virtually invisible. Rosa's user's guide lifts the covers on what's going on, what it takes to do it well, and why it works.

One final characteristic: Dynamic Facilitation is much more emergent than it may appear. At first glance, the process looks highly controlled because the facilitator is up front, calling on people and listening to them one at a time. And yet, with no agenda controlling the content, the facilitator simply supports the flow of what arises, welcoming the unexpected, the disruptive. Through the questions she asks, the gifts of everyone moved to speak are honored. Participants hear, often for the first time, from those whom they might discount in other settings. As a result, what seems a contradiction—expressing individual desires when collective action is needed—becomes a pathway for coming together. Shared meaning and actions emerge.

So if you see yourself as an agent of change, drawing forth possibilities intrinsic in complex situations, you've come to the right place. I hope, like me, you find that this user's guide gives you both the theoretical and practical information you need to do Dynamic Facilitation.

Peggy Holman
Author, *Engaging Emergence: Turning Upheaval into Opportunity*
and Co-author, *The Change Handbook*
May 8, 2013

PREFACE

In 2000, my friend Tom Atlee invited me to attend a Dynamic Facilitation workshop taught by Jim Rough, the creator of this innovative approach. Initially, I was somewhat resistant. My experience up to that point with group facilitation, the process of helping groups work together more effectively, had not been very inspiring. Many people compare working with groups to "herding cats." Most of the approaches to facilitation I had seen or experienced appeared very focused on getting people to "color inside the lines." However, Tom insisted, and I will be eternally grateful that he did so. I discovered that this new approach to group facilitation was extremely creative, powerfully transformational, and (with very few exceptions) utterly unlike anything I have encountered before or since.

Jim's work originated in an industrial setting, in which he was helping production teams find creative answers to the practical and logistical problems they were facing. He wanted to help people apply their creativity to practical issues in the workplace, including issues that may be emotionally charged, with people highly invested in their own (often conflicting) perspectives.

Over time, practitioners have discovered that Dynamic Facilitation can be used effectively for a broader range of applications. Since 1994, participants in Jim's experiential seminars have been learning this method by facilitating small-group explorations of a host of human issues, including homelessness, drug abuse, the health care crisis, etc. In the process, we have learned a lot about the power of a creative approach to help groups address community and social issues.

With Jim's encouragement, I first wrote an in-house manual on Dynamic Facilitation in 2002. Ever since then, we have been doing our best to share this work with others. We feel strongly that one of the greatest needs in our world today is for everyone to have access to effective ways of working creatively with conflicting perspectives.

Some of the details of how this journey has been unfolding, especially the growth of this work in Europe, can be found in the Acknowledgments section at the end of this book. And now, here we are—publishing this manual you are now reading with the intention of sharing this work with ever-widening circles.

INTRODUCTION

Who is this manual for? You may be interested in this work if you are:

- A professional facilitator, mediator, or consultant who is open to exploring new ways of working with groups
- A layperson interested in learning to facilitate creative group dialogue and/or practical group breakthroughs
- Someone who is engaged in an ongoing exploration of self-organization, creativity, collective intelligence, and transformation

Many of us have found Dynamic Facilitation helpful in a wide variety of contexts: with family, friends and neighbors, and community members, as well as in our professional lives. This different way of listening can make it easier for us to become more curious and interested whenever we encounter differences. It also helps us to tap into and draw out people's desire to contribute. As a result, we can help transform conflicts into creative explorations.

Many professional practitioners have found Dynamic Facilitation extremely helpful in their work. At the same time, I would also like to encourage and support DF's widespread use as a lay practice. I believe this to be a very realistic possibility, given that many people today have been developing the basic skills and mind-sets that are foundational for this approach to facilitation.

As I see it, these foundational skills and mind-sets include:

- Listening deeply and well to others
- Being willing to take *all* sides
- Trusting, allowing, and following an emergent process
- Having enough self-understanding to be able to get out of the way

Many laypeople active in self-help, personal development, and spiritual growth practices have already developed a strong foundation in these skills. This includes practitioners of Focusing, Non-Violent Communication, Empathic Listening, and other such practices. Dynamic Facilitation offers a way that these skills can be put to use for the purpose of helping groups arrive at shared understanding and creative breakthroughs on challenging practical issues.

My own background includes training and experience with Focusing practice (http://www.focusing.org) as well as earlier work with Re-evaluation Counseling. Over time, I have realized that these listening and presencing skills were key to the ease with which I subsequently learned Dynamic Facilitation. Now I recommend Focusing practice as a solid foundation for anyone, lay or professional, who wants to deepen their skills in this approach to group facilitation.

For many years now, I've held a vision of deepening our social capacity for creative collaboration by developing extensive peer networks, where laypeople trained in facilitation are able to offer a safe and effective container for groups. It is inspiring to see other initiatives sprouting up with similar aims of increasing our social capacity for meaningful and productive conversations. As practitioners of Dynamic Facilitation, we have our own particular gifts to offer to this larger field.

At the same time, I want to add a note of caution. To support sustainable change, it is not enough to be able to help a group enter and remain in a creative and transformative flow. Every group forms part of a larger organization or network. As a result, if we want our work to be sustainable, it is crucial that we develop the skills to work effectively with larger systems and their leaders.

Therefore, if you would like to practice Dynamic Facilitation professionally, you will benefit from a much broader practical knowledge set than what is included here. If you are already trained as a consultant, chances are good that you already have much of this knowledge, some of which I touch on in Chapter 3. If you do *not* have this kind of training already, I want to emphasize that the larger topic of system-wide change is not the main subject of this manual, and there is much more to learn than what I have been able to include here.

Nonetheless, the ability to help a group enter into and remain in a creative and generative flow is a significant and valuable gift in its own right. While it's only a part of the larger puzzle, I am confident that we will benefit as a society from having many more people developing skills and confidence in this area.

CHAPTER ONE

Foundations and Connections

History and Overview of Dynamic Facilitation

Jim Rough first created Dynamic Facilitation while working as a quality consultant with teams of hourly employees at a sawmill. As a way to help work teams address "impossible-to-solve" problems, he designed a process to help teams tap into their creativity and arrive at practical solutions through collective aha moments, otherwise known as breakthroughs (Rough 2002a, 2002b, 1997, 1991).

One characteristic of this approach is the ease of follow-through that accompanies the outcomes or action items that emerge in this manner. Implementation is rarely an issue, given the high energy and commitment that are a natural part of the group's shared discoveries.

When Jim began to teach his approach to group facilitation, a further application became evident. Since Dynamic Facilitation works by evoking genuine shifts of mind and heart, Jim did not want to use role-play. And since participants at his seminars came from a wide variety of settings, the only real issues they shared in common were larger human issues. Therefore, Jim began asking his students to work in groups on human issues, such as homelessness, the AIDS crisis, and abortion, in order to practice their facilitation skills during the seminars.

The usefulness of this process for hosting conversations on difficult social issues soon became apparent. One strength of Dynamic Facilitation is its ability to work with participants as they are—it does not ask people to adhere to an advanced set of ground rules, nor does it require participants to learn new ways of communication in order to engage with one another. Instead, the facilitator's very active yet non-directive role welcomes participants' advocacy, while at the same time creating the container for transformation.

While the Dynamic Facilitation process is not complicated, it does require facilitators to learn a completely different mind-set than the one conventionally assumed in attempting to "manage" the process of a meeting. For example, in Dynamic Facilitation, we do not try to persuade participants to stick to the topic. Instead, participants are supported in addressing whatever issue is of most concern to them in the moment.

I often compare this experience to a family sitting around the dinner table working on a very large jigsaw puzzle. Someone might be working on the clouds, someone else might be working on the tree line, while yet another person might be working on the building. However, as each participant contributes his or her piece, the larger picture becomes clearer and clearer.

While the facilitator is not attempting to guide or steer the process, he or she is very active and present, listening deeply to each participant in turn, actively drawing out contributions, and (heresy of heresies!) actively welcoming initial solutions. In addition, the facilitator is creating a shared map by recording all of the various ideas, perspectives, problem statements, and concerns.

As participants experience being fully heard, their focus naturally begins to expand. Instead of needing to remain narrowly focused on their initial perspective, their attention is now freed to begin exploring the larger picture that is unfolding. As each person's intrinsic motivation to discover meaningful patterns, to make sense of conflicting information, and to create new possibilities begins to emerge, participants begin to spark off each other's creative efforts.

Throughout, the facilitator encourages a diversity of perspectives. He or she holds space not just for new ideas, but also for concerns about solutions that others have proposed. Everything is included within the creative space. As a result, whenever collective aha moments emerge, they have already been shaped and refined by the group's best thinking.

Perhaps most importantly, as the process unfolds, participants naturally become more curious and welcoming of difference, since they have begun to experience that difference as a rich source for greater creativity. Each participant's unique and individual perspective is contributing to the power of the larger shared experience.

Similarities and Differences with Other Approaches

Dynamic Facilitation is an approach for working with small groups that has systemic implications. Due to its emphasis on facilitating emergence, it shares some underlying assumptions with large-group processes such as Open Space Technology and World Café that are also designed for fostering emergence (Holman, 2010; Holman, Devane, and Cady, 2007.) In Germany, where there is currently the most growth in DF practitioners, many consultants who practice OST, World Café, and Genuine Contact have been expanding their offerings to include Dynamic Facilitation.

There are other approaches to small-group facilitation, such as Bohmian Dialogue and T-groups, that also follow the "emergent process" of a group. While valuable in their own right, these approaches have *not* been designed for the specific purpose of addressing practical issues. On the other end of the spectrum, many problem-solving approaches that *are* designed to help groups address practical difficulties and challenges do *not* utilize emergent process. Instead, they usually rely on structured agendas, pre-determined sequences of steps, and negotiated decisions. In the language of agile programming methods, this conventional approach to problem-solving is called the "waterfall" approach (Culmsee and Awatii, 2011).

In contrast to most problem-solving approaches, Dynamic Facilitation welcomes both initial solutions as well as alternative problem definitions. Participants are encouraged to participate in non-linear, creative explorations where group "ahas" can occur. The purpose of these explorations is to help people discover creative and practical approaches to their most challenging issues. This can include anything from, "How do we design a better workplace?" to "How do we address the homeless problem in our community?"

In the process of arriving at new and creative solutions in a non-directive manner, participants often arrive at better interpersonal understandings. Yet the main function of Dynamic Facilitation is not to explore interpersonal relationships but to help participants generate a much deeper shared understanding of the larger system of which they are a part, which includes all of their multiple perspectives and considerations. As they do so, participants are supported in entering a co-creative mindset. As a result, they are able to discover new ways forward with regard to their initial challenges (Zubizarreta, 2013).

In addition to its affinity with large-group processes that foster emergence, Dynamic Facilitation also has some underlying affinity with Appreciative Inquiry (AI). Unlike AI, we do not hesitate to talk about problems and solutions. Yet many people have remarked that our commitment as facilitators to continually welcome and value each person's contribution to a conversation, no matter how divergent it may appear, truly embodies an appreciative spirit.

At the same time, our commitment to meeting people where they are means that we welcome participants' bringing up problems they are experiencing, just as they perceive them. We then follow up by inviting a shift from present difficulties to desired possibilities, actively eliciting the person's own solution with the question, "What would *you* do about this issue, if you were the person in charge?" In this way, our work also has some similarities with Solution-Focused approaches.

Dynamic Facilitation also has some similarities to group facilitation practices derived from the Transformative Mediation model (Bush and Folger, 2004). We share the principle of actively refraining from managing or negotiating convergence at the group level, choosing to follow the process instead of directing it. Yet we differ in our emphasis on the need to "protect" participants in order to create a safe container for creativity (Zubizarreta, 2006).

Finally, Dynamic Facilitation bears strong structural resemblances to Dialogue Mapping, a computer-assisted version of cognitive mapping (Culmsee and Awati, 2012; Conklin, 2005). Both Dynamic Facilitation and Dialogue Mapping find it useful to welcome initial solutions, concerns, new problem statements, and data, in whatever order they may appear. In Dynamic Facilitation, we track participants' contributions in a very low-tech way, using chart paper and markers to create numbered lists. In contrast, Dialogue Mapping uses Compendium, a powerful open source shareware program, to create a very organized logic map of the nonlinear conversation. This is particularly useful for handling large amounts of detailed information. As a result, some of us have begun combining these two approaches.

While acknowledging all of these various affinities and parallels, I also want to emphasize Dynamic Facilitation's own distinct tradition and the unique contributions that it offers in its own particular niche. As you are reading this manual, I encourage you to temporarily suspend what you already know and attempt to encounter this material with a fresh and open mind. Remember that the parts that may feel the most unfamiliar at first are also likely to be the greatest source of new understanding. Once we understand a practice in its own right, we are better able to play with it, adapting it and combining it with other approaches.

Choice-Creating Conversation

One helpful way to approach Dynamic Facilitation is to talk about what it's *for*, what the purpose of it is. Jim Rough likes to point out that there is a particular kind of conversation that is very useful for solving problems.

When we are faced with a problem or practical challenge, the best way of solving it is if we can enter into a creative way of thinking, looking at the situation from a variety of points of view and using our hearts as well as our minds as we consider what is really important to us. This is what allows us to come up with an elegant way to respond to our problem, a way forward that works for everyone and that actually helps us grow and change, not just solve the problem. The name that Jim Rough has given this kind of conversation is "choice-creating." He points out that this kind of thinking is often evoked in response to a crisis of some sort (Rough, 2002a, 1991).

Dynamic Facilitation is a way to reliably help a group enter into this kind of conversation. With choice-creating, we are clearly not talking about discussion, argument, or debate, even though all of those kinds of conversations have their merits. Even the word "dialogue" does not really fit, at least not in David Bohm's sense of the word, in which dialogue is focused primarily on understanding the nature of thought and consciousness. (Paulo Freire's approach to dialogue may be closer, as it has a clear orientation toward taking practical action in the world.) Choice-creating is also markedly different from deliberation; while deliberation clearly addresses practical issues, it usually implies a more linear, head-only process. For the same reasons, the terms "problem-solving" and "decision-making" don't really fit either.

In other writings, I have used the terms "practical dialogue" and "creative deliberation" to point to the fact that this kind of conversation has some shared features with dialogue and deliberation without quite fitting into either category, at least not the way they are currently used. While we may not have named this kind of conversation before, it is something we all experience. And it may well be what Einstein was pointing to when he said, "It is not possible to solve a problem at the same level of consciousness that created it."

In essence, choice-creating involves shifting our consciousness (and our conversation!) with regard to the problem that we are exploring. In the process of doing so, the problem changes, we change, and new creative possibilities are born.

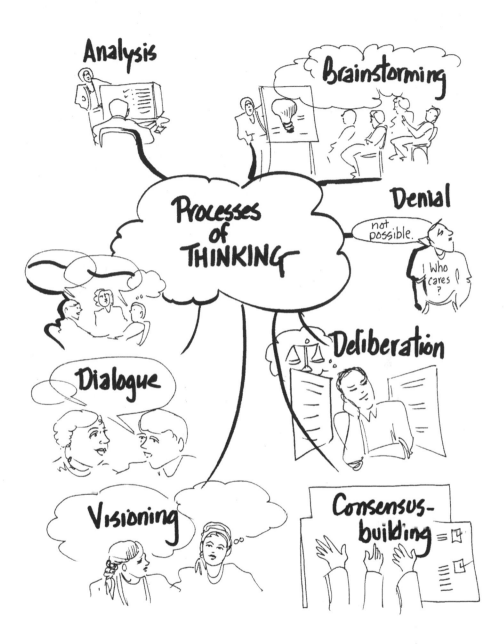

Distinguishing among different forms of thinking

The Relationship between Theory, Method, and Practice

We experience Dynamic Facilitation as a distinctive and powerful approach to group facilitation that can help groups arrive together at creative, practical, and elegant solutions to challenging issues. Since the main purpose of this manual is to help you practice and experiment with this approach, after this initial introduction I will be offering a great deal of methodological, or how-to, information.

At the same time, in the lasting words of Kurt Lewin, "There is nothing more practical than a good theory." If we understand how something works, we can creatively adapt its design, figure out when and where to use it, and even improve on the original process. On the other hand, if we simply follow a recipe, we may leave out a key ingredient and not understand the disappointing results.

Therefore, this manual includes not just a how-to, but also some thoughts about the deeper principles at work, as best as I understand them. I am not asking you to simply believe in any of the views or philosophical approaches offered here; however, I do suggest that you try them on and use them as working hypotheses.

One of the basic assumptions of this work is that our own stance as facilitators is an integral part of our practice. This includes:

- How we understand ourselves and one another
- How we understand our role as facilitators
- Our ability to trust the group's own process

All of these are, of course, related. Our stance includes not only the possibilities that we see for ourselves or for one another as individuals, but also the possibilities that we see for a group collectively.

This principle influences how we teach Dynamic Facilitation. When we lead a seminar, we do not simply offer a collection of techniques. Instead, we lead an experiential process that is designed to offer participants a different experience of what is possible in groups. To the extent that we are successful, that experience gives participants a different sense of what is possible, as well as enough confidence to continue practicing on their own. In turn, as practitioners engage in additional experiences, this confirms and deepens their sense of what is possible.

CHAPTER TWO

Basic Elements of the Facilitator's Role

What We Mean by Really Listening

In Dynamic Facilitation, the main role of the facilitator is to listen actively and deeply, creating a relational space where each participant can feel fully heard. Most importantly, this allows each participant to hear his or her own voice—to discover and bring forth their own unique perspective, what it is they truly care about. To do this, we need to take a very proactive and consistent role in supporting the emotional safety and creative contributions of each participant.

As mentioned earlier, the facilitator is *not* leading the group through any prescribed series of problem-solving steps. Instead, we are very involved on the micro-level, providing empathy, respect, and support for each participant's contribution to the shared exploration. As facilitators, we are committed to finding the gem in each participant's contribution: we are actively engaged, with relaxed yet interested curiosity.

At this micro-level, what we do in Dynamic Facilitation includes:

- Listening deeply to each participant and welcoming them just as they are (pages 15-17)
- Drawing out each participant by inviting them to say more (pages 40-41 and 43-46)
- Reflective mirroring to help each participant connect more fully with what he or she needs to say (pages 23-25)

In addition, we are:

- Actively welcoming solutions, right from the start (pages 46-47)
- Recording each participant's contribution (pages 19-21)
- Actively protecting each participant's contribution by having participants direct critical energy toward us instead of toward one another (pages 49-51)

In order to really listen, there are times when we need to actively protect participants, which may mean asking someone as respectfully as we can to wait until we have finished listening to someone else. Yet once we have done so, we need to return to that participant and make sure that his or her contribution is also deeply welcomed and received. In this way, the boundaries we are creating are in support of a deeper listening.

Conventionally, facilitators are urged to remain impartial and not take sides. Yet instead of not taking sides, it would be more accurate to describe our active and engaged facilitation role as one of taking *all* sides. This means listening deeply to each person and welcoming each perspective that is offered.

In addition to listening to individual participants, as facilitators we are also listening to the group as a whole and making room for what is newly wanting to emerge. We do this by:

- Welcoming and eliciting divergent perspectives while creating space for the co-existence of opposing views (pages 56-57)
- Refraining from steering toward convergence in any way, while holding space open for creative possibility (page 59-67)
- Providing opportunities for the group to retroactively verify or deny any apparent convergences that have emerged (pages 59-67)

To the degree that we can allow ourselves to trust in the self-organizing process (more about this on the following pages), this frees us to be continually listening for divergence and welcoming what is emerging at the edges. We are not leaning on any apparent convergence that may begin to emerge, but instead standing comfortably in the knowledge that divergent perspectives are essential for real breakthroughs.

At the same time, just as we set boundaries with individuals when we protect participants' creative contributions, we also set boundaries with the group when we help participants hold to the agreed-upon time frame for the end of the meeting. We do this by helping the group find closure at the end of the meeting.

This closure is quite different from any kind of convergence at the level of content. Instead, it has to do with creating a strong container for open-ended exploration, by honoring the time boundaries of the meeting. As part of moving to closure, we shift to helping participants organize and process the results of their exploration.

This means we are setting a boundary with regard to listening to further content. This boundary is essential for delimiting the container, to which participants can return at the next session.

Trusting and Supporting Group Self-Organization

In Dynamic Facilitation, we support the development of a self-organizing process in a group. For some people, this might seem like a contradiction in terms. Why would self-organization need any support? Yet when we think about it, we realize that life is not able to self-organize in the absence of supporting conditions. An acorn does not need anyone to tell it how to develop into an oak tree. Yet to flourish, it needs water, sunlight, and air, all in the appropriate quantities. If it does not have a sufficient amount of any of these, it will not grow. If it has less than the optimal amount, it will grow in a stunted manner.

Human beings also need some basic conditions in order to be able to grow. In addition to food, water, and air, people need to feel understood and respected by other human beings. We also need to feel that others are being authentic with us.

What does it mean to facilitate?

to elicit, sustain, and enhance Self-Organizing Change

The choice-creating perspective

Carl Rogers, the founder of humanistic psychology, described these three basic conditions for human growth and development as empathy, unconditional positive regard, and congruence. Rogers found that these conditions are both "necessary and sufficient" for supporting human self-organization in a variety of different settings, from individuals in therapy, to students in a classroom (Rogers, 1983).

In contrast, many of our institutions are still built on the model of managed change, treating humans as objects that need to be manipulated, externally motivated, regulated, and controlled. Of course, while in their pure form these two models of change are quite distinct, in reality we often see some combination of both. Yet it makes a significant difference where our center of gravity is—which form of change we see as primary.

Two basic models of change:

Managed

Self-organizing

Two paradigms - both models of change in each

The Box PARADIGM

Circle PARADIGM

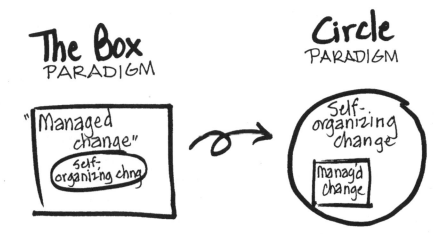

"Managed change"
Self-organizing chng

Self-organizing change
Manag'd change

Each Paradigm offers a different approach to MEETINGS

Decision-Making

CHOICE-Creating

From the perspective of choice-creating and the Circle paradigm, we see the role of facilitator as one of eliciting, sustaining, and enhancing self-organizing change. What we have found with this approach is that *when we offer empathic and respectful attention to each individual in a group, the group as a whole is able to discover its own creative and practical answers to any challenges it might be facing.* We do not need to lead the group through a linear problem-solving process nor teach them a series of communication tools in order for the self-organizing process to take place. While these tools can be valuable in their own right, they are not required for this work—just as we do not require participants to be at any particular level of consciousness for the process to be effective.

One of the useful benefits of Dynamic Facilitation is that it allows leaders to have a safe experience of the benefits of greater participation and collaboration. From the perspective of managed change, it can seem that there are only two choices: either having the leader be "in control," or else having everything be "out of control." With this kind of facilitation, we can experience the benefits of a third option.

This third option is especially valuable for leaders who want to develop greater skill with more participatory approaches to management. With Dynamic Facilitation, we include and honor the leader's own perspective, while enriching and expanding it with the perspectives of others. This creates the opportunity to directly and safely experience the power of coordinated self-organization. Jim Rough describes this use of Dynamic Facilitation as the "this, or something better…" approach, and you will read more about it in chapters three and eight.

One additional point worth mentioning here: in Carl Rogers' time, group work often included a fourth element beyond Rogers' three conditions. Some degree of confrontation was often allowed or even encouraged by the facilitator. Yet in Dynamic Facilitation, we do *not* encourage interpersonal confrontation. In fact, our emphasis on creating safety as an essential ingredient for the creative process means that facilitators actively intervene to redirect participants from confronting one another directly (pages 49-51).

To facilitate is often a breakthrough by itself

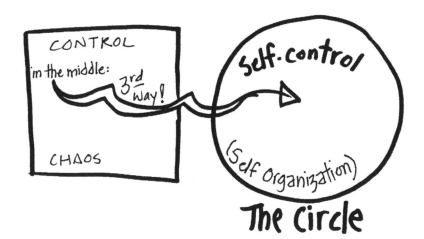

From this perspective, our aim in Dynamic Facilitation could be summarized as "minimizing interpersonal anxiety, while maximizing creative tension." We maximize creative tension by creating the conditions that allow each person to safely "confront" the wide range of perspectives that are present in the room, and thus "confront" their own previously limited perspectives. One of the ways we do this is by recording each participant's contribution—the subject of our next section.

Recording Participants' Contributions

In Dynamic Facilitation, a key aspect of our work is recording each participant's contributions as an extension of listening deeply and reflecting back what one has heard. Contributions are recorded on chart paper set up on easels so that they are visible to everyone. Seeing one's words written down offers participants the opportunity to self reflect and fine-tune what they are attempting to express.

As we do this, we create an ongoing map of the emerging dialogue, including the full diversity of perspectives contained in the group. This includes different views of what the real problem is as well as what we should really be talking about. It also includes all of the quick fixes, pet theories, and creative solutions that participants bring with them as they walk in the door, as well as participants' concerns about one another's solutions. We also write down all of the data, information, perspectives, and beliefs that each participant deems relevant.

In other words, we are not attempting to write down only the areas of convergence, but rather, to create a map of the whole landscape by recording in full each participant's contribution. In general, contributions can be understood in terms of one or more of the following categories:

Problem statements or creative challenges: "How do we...fix this machine...create better relationships...find a new market for this product...increase our family income?" In other words, how can we find or create X (our desired outcome)?

Solutions or creative contributions: Reorganize the department, take a communications training class to become better listeners, create a family circus and take it on the road.

Concerns*:* "That solution will never work, because of X." Concerns are often generated in response to others' proposed solutions.

Data*/*Perspectives: A miscellaneous category that can include complaints about what's not working, information about the larger context that affects the current situation, and statements about participants' beliefs or perceptions, etc.

Each chart is dedicated to one of these categories. So, for example, all of the solutions, regardless of when they are proposed, would go on the solutions chart. That chart contains a numbered list of items, and each solution becomes a new item on the list. Since we are recording everything (*not* just items on which there is group agreement!), each list can consist of many pages. Whenever we fill a page, we begin a new one.

Using the charts serves as a way for the facilitator to welcome, value, and track any and all contributions as they are offered, regardless of subject matter. It's also important to note that *the facilitator does not attempt to control the order in which these contributions occur, nor to keep the group focused on any particular subject area.* Instead, he or she is listening fully to each participant, reflecting contributions both orally and in writing, and helping to draw out each participant's contribution more fully.

Using the Charts to Maintain an Open Flow

Each chart consists of a numbered list of items. We are not asking the group to decide on any particular problem statement. We are also not asking the group to focus on exploring the pros and cons of any particular solution. Instead, we are listening deeply to each participant. As we listen, we are recording the various solutions, concerns, data, and problem statements contained within each participant's contribution, on their respective charts.

Reflective listening is key. As we draw out, reflect, and record each participant's contribution, our main intention is to offer participants the opportunity to hear themselves and connect more deeply with what they are wanting to say, beyond their first attempts and underneath their initial hesitations.

Our main purpose is to connect with and draw out each person. As we listen and invite, we often discover that beneath a participant's concern about someone else's solution is a solution of their own to offer. Or, maybe there is an altogether different problem statement ("This is what we should really be talking about…").

We don't need to worry about exactly where to place each contribution. If we are unsure, we can always ask the participant. It's also okay to write something down on two different charts. For instance, a particular contribution might be viewed as data, or it might be viewed as a concern. The main purpose of the four charts is to make room for each person's contributions, regardless of how divergent they may appear.

The numbered lists help create space for the co-existence of opposing views. Instead of attempting to reconcile differences, the facilitator simply listens deeply and makes room by adding each contribution as a new numbered item on the lists.

The charts help the group face the situation together. Everyone is working collaboratively to create the larger picture and seek solutions together, even when they are offering a concern, a different perspective, or a different take.

We are writing down the gist of something using complete sentences. We want to use participants' words as much as possible. We also want to get at what is "at the core" of what the participant is saying.

Each participant owns their own contribution. The facilitator continually verifies what he or she has written with the person who is speaking, inviting that person to offer any changes or corrections that might be needed.

The facilitator posts all of the recorded charts on the walls. That way, the group begins to get a clearer picture of all of the various creative challenges, solutions, concerns, and information that is in the room.

Differences between Dynamic Facilitation and Brainstorming
By this point, some readers may well be wondering, how is this different from brainstorming (or mind mapping, for that matter)? While both brainstorming and Dynamic Facilitation are designed to help people be creative in a group context, there are some key differences between the two approaches. In Dynamic Facilitation:

We take time to listen to each person in depth and make an effort to help draw out his or her perspective fully. This is very different from the rapid pace of traditional brainstorming. You might think of Dynamic Facilitation as evoking "heart creativity" as distinct from the "head creativity" evoked by brainstorming (Rough, 1991).

We welcome any concerns that people may have about one another's ideas and solutions. In brainstorming, safety is created by asking people to refrain from commenting on one another's ideas and suggestions. In Dynamic Facilitation, we also create safety for participants' creative contributions; however, we do so in a different way. We ask participants to direct their critical comments to the facilitator, instead of toward one another. This allows us to welcome and listen deeply to any concerns that participants may have about one another's ideas.

We encourage and support participants to stay in a creative space throughout the entire meeting. In other facilitation approaches, brainstorming is often used as a technique for stimulating creative thinking during the early part of a meeting. Later on, the facilitator would draw on other techniques to help the group move toward agreement. In contrast, with Dynamic Facilitation, our approach is consistent: whether at the beginning or end of a meeting, we continually welcome divergence.

We welcome any convergences that occur spontaneously as part of the creative process. However, at no point do we attempt to move the group toward agreement. Whenever it appears that the group has converged, our role is to help disprove the apparent convergence by making sure that people have the opportunity to share any concerns they may have. If it's a real breakthrough, it will remain standing.

"We-flection" and the Role of Designated Listener

The recording function we have just described can be seen as creating a written mirror or reflection for each contribution. The numbered charts created in this manner hold the non-linear map of everything that is in the room. Less tangible than the written reflections, yet maybe even more powerful, are the verbal mirroring reflections that the facilitator offers. These verbal reflections play a key role in drawing out and fine-tuning participants' contributions.

Jean Rough, Jim Rough's wife and facilitation partner, came up with the term "we-flection" to emphasize how both the facilitator and the participant work together to support the participant's process of creative self-discovery. Sometimes, when the facilitator sees that the participant is struggling to give voice to something, the facilitator may reflect back his or her best guess as to what the participant is attempting to say. If our attempt does not turn out to be correct, we will, of course, not write it down; we want the charts to reflect the participant's intended meaning. If we have written something and, on reflecting it back, it turns out we have misunderstood, we will change it.

A participant who has been circling around an issue may welcome our attempt to succinctly paraphrase the gist of his or her message: "Yes, that's it! That's exactly what I was trying to say!" Or instead, they may alter and modify our guess in some way so that it fits better. Yet even when our attempt is clearly off, and the participant responds with a "No, that's *not* it!" that too can serve as a useful stepping-stone for the participant to get clearer on what they are wanting to say.

An experienced facilitator may notice his or her own curiosity about what is being expressed and offer what he or she is hearing underneath the words. This can be quite helpful at times for participants. However, when beginning this practice, it is important to use restraint. We want to make sure that we are offering people enough time and enough silence to find their own words, instead of attempting to fill up the space with our own.

It is also important not to try too hard. Beginners sometimes make great efforts to produce complex paraphrases, when sometimes what is most valuable is to reflect back the participant's *own* words. This is especially true when a participant has already found words and phrases that have heart and meaning. In that situation, the facilitator's misguided attempt to be helpful by paraphrasing the participant's contribution will generally be experienced as a hindrance rather than a help. The participant is likely to show some signs of frustration and will often end up repeating their original words. An attentive facilitator will notice this, take the hint, and reflect and record the participant's own words, as the best way to acknowledge and honor the contribution.

We-flection, Dynamic Facilitation's elaboration on active listening, is key to the facilitator's role as designated listener. The facilitator as designated listener is the first of three main roles that the facilitator plays in Dynamic Facilitation; the other two could be described as facilitator as creativity evoker and facilitator as creativity protector. More details on how we carry out these roles can be found in Chapter 5.

Facilitator as designated listener does not mean that the facilitator is the only one listening in the room. On the contrary, the facilitator's efforts to connect with and reflect back what each participant is saying make it easier for others in the group to hear each person's offering. In appreciation of this aspect of the facilitator's role in Dynamic Facilitation, Matthias zur Bonsen has coined the term "walking talking stick." When the facilitator is listening to someone, that person is free to explore the fullness of what they might want to communicate, just as if they were holding a physical talking stick.

In addition to helping a person be heard by others, the facilitator as walking talking stick also supports each participant to "listen inside" and connect more deeply with their own inspiration. This is done through the practice of we-flection, which we have described above. Those familiar with Focusing will see how that practice can be so helpful here, as listening and offering reflections are a key element in Focusing practice. What we call reflection is also very similar to the third step in NVC Mediation's practice of empathy: "meeting the other in language where they are."

When we offer a reflection, we do our best to mirror both the content and the affect of what we are hearing. When we mirror back the emotional content in an accepting manner, it signals that emotions are welcome here. In this and in other ways, the nuances of how we listen and how we reflect serve to communicate our willingness to accompany each participant, as well as our trust in their process.

The approach to listening we are describing here implies a very different way of understanding the world, who we are as human beings, and what it means to speak and listen. As facilitators, we are tapping into a source of receptive energy that all of us can access. Eugene Gendlin, philospher and founder of Focusing, describes it as the work of "interhuman attention." In a more poetic vein, Nelle Morton wrote about the power we have "to hear one another into being."

CHAPTER THREE

Preparing the Ground

Before the Group Meetings

Regardless of which method of facilitation we may be using, the long-term impact of any meeting is greatly affected by the amount of preparation we have been able to invest beforehand. Among other things, it is helpul to explore:

- the reasons why people want to meet
- the desired outcomes they envision
- what the consequences will be if shared understanding is not reached
- what role the work of the group will play in the larger system.

This work often takes place in conversations with the meeting sponsor or sponsors. Having individual interviews beforehand with the participants can be very helpful as well (pages 32-33).

When we are inviting people to participate in a creative process, it helps for them to know something about what the process will look like and what kinds of outcomes they can reasonably expect. Of course, the selection of the process we are going to use needs to be made based on the situation and circumstances of the group. For an exploration of when Dynamic Facilitation might be appropriate and when it might not, see pages 89-93.

Since the way that shared outcomes emerge in this process is so different from a conventional approach to decision making, one way to help participants feel more comfortable is to *frame the broader purpose of a dynamically facilitated process as the creative exploration of an issue, rather than as any kind of decision making.* Participants tend to feel more comfortable knowing that any formal decisions can be worked out afterward, using their customary process.

The number of issues that will need to be formally decided upon afterward tends to be greatly reduced as a result of engaging in the creation of shared understanding. However, it can create unnecessary anxiety and/or unrealistic expectations to overemphasize this point beforehand. It is usually preferable to allow participants to discover this for themselves.

In other situations, we may want to use choice-creating as an alternative to decision making, rather than as a preparation for it. More on this, in Chapter 6.

Setting Realistic Expectations and Time Frames

Often, when we hear about a new and powerful process, there is a human tendency to expect "magic fixes" or instant solutions. In some circumstances, it can happen that a group using Dynamic Facilitation will experience a major breakthrough early on. However, as *a general principle, we recommend a series of four sessions, each between two and three hours long and usually not more than a week apart.* This ensures enough time for participants to:

- Develop a shared understanding of the complexity of the larger context, including the various perspectives held by different group members
- Enter into a creative process together
- Arrive at shared breakthroughs that clarify the shared context, uncover effective and creative solutions to practical challenges, and spell out the next steps to take to move forward with those solutions
- Reflect upon the process and what has been learned with regard to communication and collaboration

By the end of four sessions (which can be held back to back, such as in a two-day strategic planning retreat), a group will have had the opportunity to fully engage in the creative experience and to harvest the fruits of that immersion. Each member will have gained a systemic understanding of the group situation on a visceral and experiential level. Along with their shift in perspective, they will have accomplished a great deal with regard to practical outcomes, including a clear sense of their next steps and how to move forward.

The above recommendation assumes a group size of anywhere between five and twenty people. There are also ways of working with much larger groups, such as the Wisdom Council or the Creative Insight Council (Chapter 8) where we begin by working with a microcosm of the larger whole.

Of course, it can also be valuable for groups to experience a taste of choice-creating conversation, even when there is a more limited time frame. How much can be accomplished within a shorter time frame will depend on a variety of other factors, including where the group is at in relationship to understanding and engaging the real issues, as well as the facilitator's skill level and familiarity with the group.

Exploring the Broader Organizational Context

It is a great asset to have a tool that can help a group of people think together creatively and systemically so that they can arrive at powerful shared understandings and practical breakthroughs. However, when working with a group that is part of a larger organization, there are a number of broader consulting issues to consider.

Build shared understanding with key decision makers beforehand and throughout the process. Known in the consulting world as "contracting," this becomes even more essential when working with a transformational approach that brings up difficult issues and invites people to engage authentically and creatively. My own checklist of crucial conversations to have with a potential client includes the following key points:

Clarify the role and purpose of the facilitated meetings within the larger organizational context. When people are invited to open up, and then there is no opportunity for real follow-through, the effect can be worse than zero. Of course, if we are in a position where we can continue to work with a group on an ongoing basis, then how to get their ideas utilized can become the next creative challenge. In that case, how decision makers respond initially does not need to be an issue.

However, for short-term engagements, the larger context is crucial. This is especially important in the case of public participation projects, where it is not only employee morale but the larger public trust that is at issue. In a nutshell, one of the biggest disappointments for a group is to engage in a series of highly productive meetings only to have their work be ignored or disregarded.

Understand the real bottom line in terms of leaders' desired outcome(s). As explored more fully in the final chapter on applying Dynamic Facilitation, there are no methods that will be ethically appropriate in situations where the client is seeking the appearance of consent. However, in situations where a decision has already been made, it is still possible to move forward constructively, as long as we begin with a full disclosure followed by an exploration of "this or something better," as described more fully on pages 91-92.

Yet even when a decision has *not* been made, leaders will naturally have their own initial solution ideas, which they need to disclose early on for maximum effectiveness. Even when key leaders are genuinely open to the process, it can sometimes take quite a bit of one-on-one listening and coaching beforehand to help them feel confident enough to share their own hopes, fears, and desired outcomes. It is essential that we take the time to do this, as it prepares leaders to participate fully and effectively in the process.

"Purge the boss first!" Sometimes in facilitated meetings, leaders have a well-intentioned yet counterproductive tendency to either not participate in the process at all or to hold back in a misguided effort to encourage broader participation. In the context of Dynamic Facilitation, this is the last thing we want. It does not serve anyone for the facilitator to encourage group creativity only to have everyone's bubble burst as, toward the end of the meeting (or worse, after the meeting), the leader finally reveals the bottom-line constraints that make the group's work useless or irrelevant.

Instead, we need to let the meeting sponsors know beforehand that during the meeting we will be drawing them out *first* to get their contribution out on the table. In this way, group creativity can emerge within the context of all of the known parameters. It's often useful to explain to leaders that it's most helpful for the group if they, as leaders, can model full participation, rather than simply advocating that others participate fully while they themselves hold back.

However, simply saying this may not be enough. I still recall a situation where, three-quarters of the way through a meeting, I was surprised to see the director of a nonprofit pull out a long list of issues that he wanted the group to address. Although we had spent quite a bit of time in preparation before the meeting, there had been no mention of this list, nor any of the items on it!

The point of this story is to highlight how essential it is to draw out the meeting sponsor in advance of working with the group, and also to point out how challenging this can be. Our goal is to build enough trust so that leaders can share with us beforehand what it is that they truly want and need. We can then invite the leaders to share that information with the rest of the group early on in the process.

We also need to let leaders know that our effectiveness as facilitators depends upon being able to keep participants from being interrupted, even by (especially by!) the leaders themselves. Of course, leaders are welcome to offer their concerns in response to others' solutions, just like anyone else. However, in advance of the meeting, our work is to help leaders understand how destructive it can be for them to interrupt a participant's solution with the equivalent of "been there, done that, won't work." Even if a solution is in fact completely inadequate, our job as facilitators is to create a situation where participants can save face and remain creative by realizing this on their own. Also, every inadequate solution can serve as a catalyst for other, more effective solutions if we, as facilitators, are able to do our work of maintaining an environment that encourages individual creativity.

At any point during these initial conversations, either the facilitator, the meeting sponsors, or both may realize that this situation is not a good fit. In fact, this is one of the central goals of contracting: to explore the degree of fit that is possible by being honest with ourselves and with our client.

Get a preview of the real issues at play. Dynamic Facilitation's focus on authenticity means that we are opening a space to engage with whatever is really going on, especially since there is no preset agenda to keep us from talking about the real issues.

In preparation, it can be helpful to begin by conducting individual interviews with group members. If we are not able to interview everyone, we can choose a diverse selection, making sure to include anyone who might be identified by others as particularly challenging. These individuals may be serving as scapegoats and often have valuable perspectives to contribute regarding unaddressed issues.

The purpose of these interviews is four-fold:

- Establish trust with individual group members
- Begin to develop a sense of the issues and the larger context
- "Prime the pump" for participants by offering them an opportunity to think aloud ahead of time
- Introduce the process to group members, not just descriptively but experientially, through our listening and reflection during the interviews

When conducting the interviews, these are the kinds of questions I ask:

- What is working well?
- What isn't?
- What do you see as key problems or challenges here?
- What would you do about that particular challenge if it were up to you?
- How willing are you to share your perspective with the group as a whole?
- What issues might you hesitate to bring up in the group because they seem too hopeless or difficult?

Once I have conducted the interviews, I offer a courtesy feedback session to the meeting sponsors. While careful to maintain individual confidentiality, I review the general themes that have come up, ask the leader how comfortable he or she is with having these issues surface in a group setting, and offer supportive coaching as needed. *The basic principle is to create safety by minimizing surprises.*

CHAPTER FOUR

Getting Started

Introducing the Process

To introduce a Dynamic Facilitation process to a group, it's best to begin with a brief description of the purpose and tone of the process, the role of facilitator, and some clear requests regarding what you are asking of participants.

Each of us will find our own preferred way of doing this. When I am facilitating, I often begin by:

Letting participants know that this process is designed to help us develop a big-picture understanding of a situation, to better arrive at shared outcomes. As a creative process, it may feel somewhat unfamiliar or messy at times.

Using the analogy of a jigsaw puzzle to describe how we might jump around a bit as we explore various issues. I reassure the group that with time, as we place all the various pieces, a more coherent picture will begin to take form.

In describing my own role, I like to:

Explain that as facilitator, I am only able to listen to one person at a time. As such, I will need to ask people to take turns.

Emphasize that I will be listening to each person fully before proceeding to the next person. I acknowledge that this is different than usual and may try their patience at times. I also let participants know that my intention is to hear from each person, and then I ask for their help in making sure this happens.

Let participants know that to protect each person's creative contributions, I will be asking them to direct any charged comments to me as the facilitator. I model what this looks like by selecting two participants, walking over to stand right between them, and asking them to please direct their comments to me.

In describing participants' roles, I like to:

Invite participants to be themselves and remind them that their individual contributions are key to the process. This is *especially* true whenever they are feeling particularly out of step with the rest of the group. Their own unique perspective may well turn out to be the missing piece of the puzzle, even though at first it might not seem to fit with the rest of the picture.

Invite participants to own the charts. It's their role to help make sure that whatever I write is an accurate reflection of their contributions.

Invite participants to pay attention to their feelings as valuable information. While there is no expectation that they share their feelings in a group setting and each person's privacy will be respected, participants are welcome to bring in that dimension of their experience to the extent they are comfortable doing so.

The above eight points are usually sufficient for introducing the process to a group. If I have interviewed individual participants before the first meeting, I will have already gone over some of these points. Even so, I generally review the entire process again with the group as a whole at the beginning of the first meeting.

Sometimes it may be important to introduce other considerations, such as agreements around the confidentiality of what will be shared in the room. For example, if community members are coming together to explore a polarized situation, it can be important for everyone to agree that what will be shared in the room will stay in the room. Participants can agree to only talk about their own experiences afterward, not about who said what.

In some situations, such as when people do not already know one another, it often makes sense to begin the meeting by going around the circle before describing the Dynamic Facilitation process. For example, we might invite people to introduce themselves and share their own hopes and concerns for this meeting. While it can take a while to complete this kind of circle check-in, it is well worth the effort. It helps create a basic sense of safety and gives each person an opportunity to truly arrive.

Once everyone has gone around the circle and introduced him or herself, we can then talk about the process we will be using for the meeting, as described above. That way, there is not too large a time lapse between our description of the process and when we actually begin engaging in it.

What about Ground Rules?

In Dynamic Facilitation, we value being able to meet people where they are, instead of asking them to behave differently or to censor themselves. Therefore, instead of using ground rules in an attempt to create safety, we emphasize active facilitation and modeling. As the saying goes, "attitudes are caught, not taught." As a facilitator listens deeply to participants, he or she is modeling good listening. Even more importantly, the facilitator is helping participants feel heard. In the process, participants naturally become more able and willing to listen to others.

Of course, this approach takes time. In the meantime, the facilitator is actively intervening to protect participants whenever necessary. For example, if someone interrupts, the facilitator might say, "Excuse me, I really want to listen to what you are saying, but first I want to make sure that I have finished hearing this person." When the facilitator finishes with the first person, he or she will turn back to the one who interrupted to listen and draw out that person's contributions in full. Or, depending on the circumstances, the facilitator might redirect attention to someone who is in obvious distress and then come back to the person who was originally speaking. Regardless, the larger point is that it is the facilitator's job to hear each person fully, and this will inevitably require some turn-taking.

Sometimes our role as facilitator will require us to walk up and place ourselves physically between two participants in order to interrupt a heated back-and-forth. In such a situation, we might say, "I really want to hear what each of you is saying. But I can only listen to one person at a time, so I will need to ask you to take turns." Then we invite each participant to redirect his or her heat toward us as facilitators instead of toward one another. In this way, people are able to speak truth openly, overhear one another, and experience safety in a group setting.

Usually, describing and modeling this process is enough for participants to feel comfortable. Yet on a few occasions I've worked with groups that insisted on creating ground rules, since that is how they were used to working. I've responded by being flexible and going along with this, yet I've also engaged participants in a conversation about what each of their proposed rules mean to them. In this way, the conversation becomes an opportunity to build trust and greater understanding of one another.

Even when a group has chosen to create ground rules, I do not see my role as enforcer of the rules. Instead, my responsibility is to facilitate in a way that generates shared understanding, the valuing of diverse perspectives, and synergy. And I've found that when we do so, most "rules" become unnecessary, beyond the simple role descriptions offered in the previous section.

Beginning the Content Exploration: Do We Need an "Issues" Page?

In many situations, the purpose of a meeting is fairly clear. For instance, a team has been encountering some difficulties, and someone has arranged for a consultant to come in. Ideally, we've conducted individual interviews with group members beforehand; if not, we have at least had extensive conversations with the meeting sponsor(s) to understand their intentions and desired outcomes.

Of course, even though there is a shared difficult situation, each person in the group will have his or her own take on what the real problem is. Yet even if each person defines it quite differently, they are all pointing in the same general direction: "That mess over there, which results in these kinds of troubles…" That is usually enough initial clarity for us to begin. In these kinds of situations, we can start by just jumping in, as described on the following page.

Yet in some situations (such as a public DF workshop, where participants are there to learn DF, yet do not share a common organizational background) there may be a number of different issues that a group could choose to address. In that case, we may want to help the group create an issues page and choose an issue before we invite them to jump in.

To do this, we begin by having the group generate a list of possible issues. Then we work together to select one, keeping in mind that the Dynamic Facilitation process has been designed to work best for issues that people care a lot about, and for which they have a lot of energy or passion. This is true even if (or maybe especially if) they are currently at odds or polarized on the subject.

On the other end of the spectrum, Dynamic Facilitation also works very well for "impossible-to-solve" problems about which people may be feeling quite hopeless instead of energized. These seemingly impossible-to-solve problems require real creativity in order to find a solution. In these kinds of situations, the confidence and experience that the facilitator brings can be key for encouraging participants to be willing to tackle these kinds of challenges.

If the group needs to work on routine tasks, or things for which no creativity is needed, Dynamic Facilitation may not be the best method for them to use. However, if the group has a good block of time available, it could be a good opportunity to choose one of those difficult issues that too often remains unaddressed because people feel too hopeless about the possibility of making any real progress.

Jumping In

Once everyone is clear on the overall purpose of the meeting, has come together, and is willing to take part in a facilitated process, we are ready to jump in. If there is a formal leader in the group, it is generally helpful to establish the understanding that he or she will be the first participant in the facilitated process (see "purge the boss first" on pages 31-32) so they can lay out the parameters of the situation as they see it, along with their own best solution to date.

Or, in some situations, the first participant may simply be a person who has a great deal of energy and passion about the situation and is willing to jump in. Regardless, the procedure is as follows:

The facilitator begins with the first person, helping to draw out his or her response. Often, that person will start out by talking about what's wrong, describing the initial mess that needs to be addressed. The facilitator will reflect and record these as concerns or data.

After recording some of the features of the mess, the facilitator follows up by asking that same participant for his or her solution. The facilitator might ask, "If it were completely up to you, what would your solution be?" and record the ideas on the Solutions Chart (see pages 46-47).

When the facilitator has fully drawn out the first person, he or she turns to someone who also seems to have energy about the issue. The next participant may have a concern about the issue or about the solution offered by the first speaker. While protecting the first participant's contribution (see pages 49-51), the facilitator welcomes the concern. He or she will then draw out the second participant, inviting that participant to contribute their own best solution.

It is also possible that the second person will have a completely different perspective on what the issue is. Thus, their solution may address an entirely different implicit formulation of the problem. This is perfectly welcome; the facilitator will record that solution on the solutions list and may add both problem formulations to the problem-statement list (see pages 51-53).

Again, the facilitator helps this person to be fully heard before offering attention to the next person. By this point, the facilitator is no longer at the beginning of the meeting but well into the initial stage, described more fully in the next section.

CHAPTER FIVE

Key Aspects of the Initial Stage

From Complaints to Creativity

A question often posed to anyone teaching facilitation is, "What can you do about the people who go on and on and don't seem to want to give any-one else a turn?" Truth is, this is rarely a problem in DF. In fact, it has taken us some time to figure out what we were doing that kept this from being a problem! When I first started teaching Dynamic Facilitation, I attributed it to our intensive use of mirroring reflections, or we-flection (pages 23-25). I'd explain that we humans don't necessarily feel heard just because we've said something; often we don't feel that someone has listened to us until we hear some acknowledgement, until we have been able to hear our contribu-tion reflected back to us in an empathic and supportive manner.

I'd also point out that recording each participant's contribution on chart paper helps deepen the experience of being heard. If someone keeps repeating him or herself, we might on occasion point to where their earlier contribution has already been written down and respectfully inquire whether there is something else they would like to add. Yet the oral and written reflections, while a part of the answer, are not the whole of it.

One day, while being interviewed by a researcher who was studying emergent group processes, I finally realized the missing piece. Of course someone could go on and on…and on and on…and on and on… regardless of how much active listening they might be receiving, *if* all they were doing was complaining! In fact, empathizing could even make it worse, turning the interaction into an endless gripe fest. That's when I realized that there was a key step in our process, something we were already doing, that I had not fully recognized yet.

If someone is complaining, we listen for a full minute or two. We will reflect their complaints, write them down as data or as concerns, and listen a bit more. And then, *especially* if the person seems ready to go on and on, we might say something like this:

> "I hear that you have many serious complaints. You don't like X, and you are concerned when you see Y, and you have lots of data that proves that Z has happened, which is not a good thing at all. And it seems like there are many, many more things that you could list, that are *not* going the way they should…maybe even hundreds of them. (Here, the participant usually nods enthusiastically.)
>
> "However, it's also clear to me that you *really* don't like this situation at all, and, if it were up to you, you would *really* want something different to happen around here. So, what I'd like to ask you now is, if it were up to *you* to set things right, what is it that you would like to see happen, and how would *you* go about doing it?"

Our experience has been that whenever we invite someone to share a solution, the situation suddenly changes. We no longer need to worry about participants going on and on. Instead, people tend to become quite timid. Our challenge at this point is usually how to create enough safety and offer enough encouragement for that person to willingly share his or her answer with the group.

It's important to be clear that this is *not* a strategy to get someone to button up. Instead, we are sincerely and genuinely interested in the initial solutions that each person in the room is carrying. Welcoming initial solutions—indeed, working hard to draw them out (hence the term "purging")—is a key aspect of Dynamic Facilitation and brings with it a whole host of benefits.

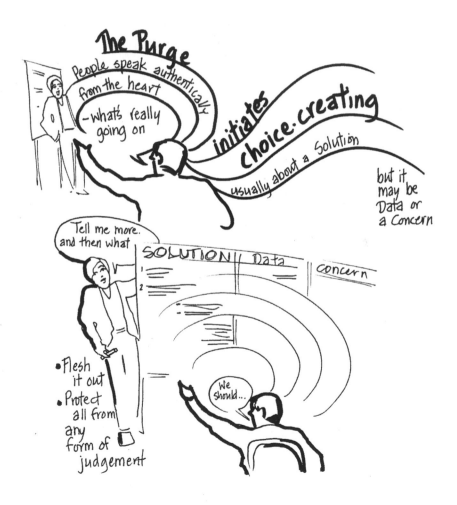

Without having seen this in practice, it's easy to remain skeptical. People often point out that the difficult person they have in mind is someone who is filled with solutions. In fact, that person is always trying to tell others what the answer is! From our perspective, however, we might wonder if that person has truly had the opportunity to feel heard by others, regardless of how much they have been talking. We might also consider that this sounds like someone who really cares about the situation and would like to improve it.

We want to honor that caring and the feelings associated with it. It is quite painful to want to contribute, and yet to sense that one's contributions are not being welcomed nor understood. At the same time, we do not simply stay at the feeling level. Asking "what would you do, if it were up to you?" and then listening with interested curiosity offers the participant an opportunity to fully articulate their ideas for moving forward.

It's quite true that people who have a pet solution are always attempting to talk about their idea. Yet without the benefit of a listening space specifically designed to welcome creativity, it's rare to encounter a receptive invitation to flesh out ideas to their logical conclusions.

As we provide that listening space by drawing out each solution and seeking to understand it to the speaker's satisfaction, and as we welcome the various concerns that emerge, we are creating a context in which new shared understandings can be generated in the group, and where repetitive patterns can begin to shift.

Honoring Creativity by Welcoming Initial Solutions

When people first arrive at a meeting, they often bring with them their own attempts to imagine what a solution might be to the shared challenges at hand. As imperfect as these initial solutions may be, limited by incomplete information and partial perspectives, they are also a rich source of data for the group. In addition, these solutions represent people's best creative efforts to date.

As facilitators, we want to support and encourage creativity. We want participants to feel heard so that they are, in turn, better able to listen to others. We want to help participants empty themselves of what they already know and look at things from new perspectives so they are able to come up with new ideas. *To accomplish all this, we have found that it is highly effective to welcome and listen deeply to participants' solutions right from the very start.*

Therefore, we do *not* ask people to wait until agreement has emerged around a problem definition before sharing solutions. Instead, whenever a participant offers a concern or points to a problem, we assume that this situation is something that this particular individual has already spent some time thinking about. As a result, *we encourage any person who has just offered a concern to also see what solution of their own might be brewing, and to share it with us.*

This can be more difficult to accomplish than it might appear. Often people will need active encouragement. *Usually, people tend to only share the tip of the iceberg. We want the whole iceberg.* This is true even when participants seem quite eager to share their ideas. If we pay close attention, we may notice that they are speaking in generalities. Even very outspoken people may need quite a bit of encouragement to become very concrete and specific here.

Yet once the facilitator has welcomed the idea, reflected it, and recorded it, it's extremely rare for someone not to feel satisfied. In truth, we do not find much difference between those who are reticent and those who are voluble. *In either case, listening to, drawing out, and acknowledging a person's favored solution helps that person develop a greater readiness to listen to others' perspectives.*

As the facilitator draws out each person, participants will naturally discover that others have different perspectives and begin to sense the larger complexity of the situation. In the process, the limitations of initial solutions will quite readily become apparent. However, it is not the facilitator's job to point out any flaws in the solutions proposed but to help each person feel heard, protect each person's creative contribution, and record all of the data that emerges.

Welcoming Both Solutions *and* Concerns

Initial solutions contain valuable information for the group, as they offer insight into participants' various perspectives. They also serve as a valuable source of raw material for the much more comprehensive solutions that emerge later, once the group has had an opportunity to digest the larger picture that is emerging. Initial solutions also serve the group by eliciting concerns from other participants.

Any concerns offered by participants in response to others' solutions are valuable sources of information for the group. In addition, underneath a participant's concern, there is often another alternative solution. The facilitator's task is to draw out the concern, as well as the alternative solution that may lie beneath it.

In general, we do not want to use concerns and alternative solutions to go back and modify the original solution proposed by someone else. Instead, it is more helpful to continue moving forward. First, we record the concern on the Concerns Chart. Then, if the concern contains an alternative solution, we add it to the list as a new solution, even if it is a modification of an existing solution. This helps protect the particular shades of meaning inherent in each person's creative efforts. Often we tend to think that two people are saying almost the same thing, yet the vitality of creative expression and complex thinking lies precisely in allowing room for apparently small but ultimately significant distinctions.

In addition to concerns and alternative solutions, participants may have a completely different take on what the real problem is. In that case, we need to draw out their own solution to the problem as they see it and add that solution to our Solutions Chart. We can also make explicit the new problem statement that this participant is addressing and add that to our Problem-Statements Chart (see pages 51-53).

Note: Once in a great while, the group may experience a real breakthrough during the initial stages of the meeting. As the facilitator is drawing each person out, the group may discover that one person's initial solution is the key for which they have been searching. That person may have attempted to offer their contribution previously without success and is only now able to be heard.

Of course, this is not usually the case. Any initial "pearls of wisdom" will usually need to be digested by the group for some time before they are made their own. It is much more likely that all the initial solutions offered by participants will end up as compost, extremely useful raw material for the group's later work. However, these early breakthroughs, while rare, are still worth mentioning.

Protecting Creativity *and* Working Effectively with Advocacy

One of the key gifts of Dynamic Facilitation is how we are able to hold space for both creative *and* critical thinking. First, a word about advocacy: our role as facilitators is to create an environment where each individual's advocacy can be a gift to the group. We do this by listening deeply to each individual's strongly held positions, reflecting, and recording each contribution. As we do so, this creates a context in which participants are more able to listen to themselves. We find that positions tend to become more nuanced as participants connect more deeply with what they are really wanting and feeling. As each participant begins to feel more heard, we find that he or she naturally begins to shift into a greater openness and curiosity about others' experiences.

At the same time, as facilitators, we need to actively protect participants' creativity from any criticism or judgment. We do this by inviting participants to direct their energy at us, while welcoming their contributions with openness and receptivity. If necessary, we will physically step in the middle of an exchange and invite each person to take turns addressing his or her concerns to us so that we can listen, reflect, and record his or her position. This allows participants in the group to listen better. Rather than needing to defend or respond to having emotional energy directed at them, they are instead able to "overhear" one another's advocacy.

Protection is especially important in a creative process whenever participants have just offered the tender creative green shoot of a new idea. In these kinds of situations, even the mildest form of criticism can feel devastating. Judgment tends to shut down the creative process by destroying the feeling of safety and triggering the need for self-protection. Especially at the beginning stages of the process, it is key for the facilitator to have participants direct any concerns about another person's solution to the facilitator rather than to the originator of the idea.

If we notice that safety may have been breached, we need to work to re-establish connection. We can do this by returning to the person who originally proposed the idea that is now being criticized. We reflect the original idea again and ask the person if we've got it. Then, after "protecting" the first person by reaffirming our understanding of their contribution, we make sure that the person with the concern offers it *directly to us,* so we can reflect and record it.

Creating a safe context to welcome advocacy allows each individual to offer his or her gift. A concern is a sign that an individual cares about the work and wants it to go well. Our role is not to dissuade concerns, only to create a space where creative thinking and critical thinking can co-exist productively.

Some individuals may need more time and support than others. When an individual is particularly loud or particularly withdrawn, greater encouragement on the facilitator's part may be required to draw out the gems that these participants are bringing to the group. Yet in the process, we often find that challenging individuals hold a particularly valuable piece of the larger puzzle.

Our role as facilitators is to meet people where they are, not to ask them to change. To the degree that change happens as part of a naturally unfolding process, we welcome it. Yet our activity is not focused on getting participants to establish or adhere to any communication guidelines beyond the practical necessity of taking turns so that we can hear each person fully.

While listening to someone, the facilitator will often notice changes in a participant's posture and body language. As individuals are given the opportunity to connect with their own thoughts and feelings more deeply and to feel fully heard and received by at least one other person, they tend to visibly relax and soften. The presence or absence of these signals can help us realize whether we need to continue in our respectful attempts to understand someone more fully or whether we have succeeded in doing so.

In later stages of the Choice-Creating Process, once all participants have "purged" and entered the zone of creative collaboration, there is a different feeling in the room, as well as a natural shift in responses to others' creative efforts. Responses will tend to be more of the "yes, *and...*" variety.

At that point, the facilitator can stand back and focus on recording. He or she will occasionally step back in to reflect and summarize, but may do so after every four or five contributions, rather than after each one.

However, at any point when it seems that there is a critical back-and-forth beginning to emerge, the facilitator will step back in to protect the creative energy by redirecting the comments toward the charts, helping to make sure that each participant is fully heard, and inviting others in the room to speak as well.

The Problem-Statements Chart: Tracking the Evolving Flow

Often, the most powerful breakthroughs in the Choice-Creating Process can take the form of a new question. Arriving at a shared sense of what the real issue is can be huge, even if we do not yet have any solutions for the new challenge. To arrive here, we need to welcome different perspectives on what the real issue is. At the same time, we also need to access our whole selves—both our logical and our creative/intuitive minds.

Toward this end, rather than attempting to logically arrive at a shared definition of the problem at the outset, what we do instead is welcome the various creative solutions that participants bring with them. Then we "back-cast" or work backward *from* those solutions, making explicit the different implicit problems or design challenges that each solution is attempting to solve.

We do this by using the Problem-Statements Chart. Here's an example: Imagine that various participants have just proposed three different solutions, all addressing an issue of timeliness with projects. As a facilitator, you might then suggest the following problem statement: "Hmm, it seems to me that many of you have been working on the question of how to get projects to come in on time."

Given the non-linear nature of creative conversation, it is likely that participants have also meandered a bit, and two other solutions have been proposed recently, both of them having to do with improving internal communications—not just with regard to the late projects, but more generally. So you might also suggest another problem statement: "It also seems like there has been some work on the question of how to improve internal communications in general. Shall I add that as another problem statement?"

If this makes sense to the group, you would add both of those questions to the Problem-Statements Chart. In this way, this chart becomes a tool for tracking the emergent flow of the group conversation—not directing it, as an agenda might, but instead simply tracking what is actually taking place. Thus, the Problem-Statements Chart is the only chart where the facilitator may be the one suggesting additions. Of course, a participant might offer a problem statement, in which case we would record that as well—and then promptly ask what *his or her own* solution to that problem statement would be.

There are three key distinctions here:

To promote creativity, we generally phrase entries on the Problem-Statements Chart as how-to questions. Since each how-to question frames a different problem or design challenge, we might also think of this as the Problem-Framing Chart, or the Design Challenge Chart.

Questions on the Problem-Statement Chart are always worded in the affirmative. In other words, we want to ask how to achieve a desired end-state rather than how to get rid of an undesirable state. Their general form, then, is "How can we create X (this particular desired end-state)?"

Just because there is a question in the room does not mean that it ends up on the Problem-Statement Chart. This chart is only for tracking questions that correspond to the solutions being generated by participants.

To illustrate this last point: imagine that in the middle of a session, someone asks, "Just exactly how many employees have we hired in the last year?" No one in the room has a satisfactory answer. And so we would capture the question on the Data Chart: "Some of us want info on exactly how many employees we have hired recently," or "Question in the room: How many employees hired last year?" or even just "How many hires last year?" If participants are interested in following up and gathering data, this could also become an action item on an Outcomes Chart (see page 80).

In other words, the Data Chart contains the data we have as well as the data we need to or want to have. The Data Chart is also an appropriate place to record any philosophical musings that participants might offer as valuable data about the various sorts of questions that participants are asking themselves. This is not intended to devalue the importance of other kinds of questions. The Data Chart contains much valuable information that is highly relevant to the group and that can be the source of powerful breakthroughs.

Again, the sole purpose of the Problem-Statements Chart is to list the various "How can we…?" questions that the various solutions already offered have been attempting to answer. Sometimes facilitators learning this approach find the metaphor of *Jeopardy* to be useful. We are harvesting participants' contributions in the form of their initial solutions—and then, back-casting to find the how-to questions that their solutions are attempting to solve.

As mentioned earlier, it may be the case that the breakthrough that emerges is in the form of a question on the Problem-Statements Chart, which everyone comes to realize is the "key" question. However, this is not necessarily the case. The breakthrough may take the form of convergence on a particular solution on the Solution Chart, or even new perspective that arises from something on the Data Chart. Regardless, the Problem-Statement Chart is extremely helpful for tracking and acknowledging shifts in the group's attention and energy.

The Data Chart: Honoring Context, Perspectives, and Everything Else
Much of the energy in a choice-creating meeting is held in the dance between solutions and concerns, the dynamic tension between creative and
critical thinking. In turn, the Problem-Statements Chart, as we have just
seen, serves as a very useful way for the facilitator to track the work the
group is doing. Yet the Data Chart also has its own gifts, which can play a
key role in the overall process.

In some ways, "data" is a misnomer. We are not necessarily talking
about scientifically verified facts. Instead, we are talking about data in a
much more colloquial sense. What goes on the Data Chart might include
any bit of information (verified or unverified) that someone in the room
deems significant. Or it may be a question someone has about some information that would be helpful to have. What goes on the Data Chart may
also be a belief, a perspective, or a feeling that someone is holding. Or, it
may be a bit of historical context that someone feels is relevant to the present situation. *In other words, anything that a participant offers that is clearly
not a solution or a concern can be recorded on the Data Chart.*

Something to watch out for is the human tendency to hide be-
hind data. As a result, *sometimes things end up on the Data Chart that are
really concerns in disguise or even solutions in disguise.* When we realize that,
we can work with the person who offered the data to see if it would be
okay to add the underlying solution or concern to the appropriate chart.
As we do so, we don't need to worry about crossing the data off the Data
Chart. It's perfectly okay for something to end up on two charts.

The main function of the Data Chart is to make sure that there is
a place for everything. In that sense, we might see it as a bit of a catchall.
Yet this should not lead us to diminish the value of the material that ends
up here.

When we are engaged in a choice-creating process, participants are
able to hear things in new ways. Sometimes the breakthrough may turn out
to be a piece of data—maybe even something that everyone already knew,
yet that now has new meaning. For example, in a team working on improvement efforts, a participant speaks up in the middle of the process. She

speaks movingly about how (from her perspective) everyone in the organization is still in mourning over the layoffs that took place six months ago.

Clearly, this is not a new piece of information, but the fact that it has been spoken into this particular context, where everyone is being deeply heard and where everyone's creativity is being welcomed, results in the emergence of a deeper shared understanding of the impact. As others speak about their own experiences, different solutions are proposed to deal with the new issue that has been introduced. At the end of this first meeting, we may not have one clear path forward among the handful of new solutions that have been proposed. At this point, the breakthrough is not something on the Solutions Chart; instead, it is the shared understanding that has emerged, the meaning that has been created with regard to this piece of data.

In addition to historical context, other kinds of data may end up having particular relevance for the group as a whole. These can include polarities or creative tensions that may be at play, real stories about past instances when things were working particularly well, and/or bits of information that may not be widely shared in the organization as a whole, yet turn out to be game changers.

As facilitators, we do not need to worry about whether or not a particular piece of data will be a game changer. Our role is to simply listen to each person, welcome their concerns, draw out the creative energy that is embodied in their solutions, and, if there is anything that does not fit onto those two charts, continue to listen deeply, welcome it fully, and write it down on the Data Chart.

Note: The purpose of the charts is to collect the information that is in the field in a way that maximizes everyone's ability to identify with it. So just as we do *not* write down names next to solution ideas nor next to concerns, we also do not write names down next to perspectives or opinions on the Data Chart. For example, after we have listened to a participant for a while, instead of writing "Harry thinks that John is an idiot," we might end up writing something like, "Some of us are extremely upset by the behavior of the sales department, as it seems impossible to make sense of what they are doing." Of course, we would also be checking in with the participant who had offered this perspective to see whether our summary statement captures their sentiment appropriately.

The major exception to not including names happens when we get to action planning (see pages 72-75) In that case, we want to make sure we *do* have names next to each item.

Drawing out Group Divergence

In Dynamic Facilitation, our most difficult challenge is drawing out participants fully so that their various perspectives can adequately inform the creative work of the group. In most social situations, there is a natural and understandable tendency for people to downplay and skirt areas of potential conflict in the interest of preserving relationships. Yet paradoxically, the human tendency to avoid and minimize conflict can also end up having a negative impact on relationships.

In a group, some individuals may choose to hold back initially, waiting to see if it is really safe before sharing their perspectives. Or, they might feel that their own views are too different from the rest of the participants'. Whenever it appears that only one side of an issue is being expressed, we may need to explicitly ask the group whether anyone present might be holding the opposite perspective.

When someone who has not spoken for a long time finally offers his or her perspective (often quite tentatively or with some hesitation), it is particularly important that the facilitator draw out that participant, reflecting and affirming their contribution. As others are able to overhear the new perspective in depth, it becomes additional information that helps the group reach a new level of thinking. As the group begins to experience how the creative process benefits from listening to unfamiliar perspectives, a sense that divergence is truly welcome starts to emerge.

Of course, a necessary element for this is our own comfort level with regard to holding apparently contradictory perspectives. We need to be able to make room for each, without any pressure to rush into a quick resolution.

It can be particularly hard to welcome divergence when we feel that the group is close to a point of convergence. Despite our best efforts, we may not realize that someone has been holding back until we attempt to verify what appears to be a group breakthrough. At that point, we may be surprised to discover that a participant has not yet voiced his or her deep concerns. While others may have entered the phase of creative synthesis, that work has not considered the perspective of the person who has not yet "purged."

Regardless of timing, the only way to move forward constructively is to accept this situation as a gift—a valuable opportunity to genuinely welcome and draw out the missing person's contribution, and then proceed with the open-ended, non-directive creative process. As the group obtains a more complete picture of the diverse perspectives contained within it, the natural process of creative synthesis will continue on a deeper level.

CHAPTER SIX

Transition and Intermediate Stages

Allowing Convergence to Emerge

Many facilitation approaches include a variety of techniques to help draw out divergence. If you are a professional facilitator, what we have described so far could appear to be simply a novel way for helping bring forth the divergence that is already present in the group.

Yet the radical gift of Dynamic Facilitation is that *we never shift gears to lead a group into convergence.* Instead, we help a group remain within the creative process so that any convergences that emerge can do so spontaneously.

While we do not lead a group through steps, we do find that groups tend to move, of their own accord, through a series of stages. One pattern we usually encounter is the shift from:

- the Purge Stage, where people are sharing what they already know, to

- the Yuck Stage, a *brief* transition period in which participants usually feel overwhelmed, wondering how they will reconcile all the different perspectives, to
- the Group Flow Stage of excitement over creative possibilities, during which the group experiences an ongoing cycle of divergence-convergence-divergence etc., as the spontaneous unfolding of the creative process, to
- the Commitment Stage, where participants want clear action steps.

In the first stage, the facilitator is purging people of what they already know by drawing them out, helping them feel heard, and recording their contributions. When dealing with a large issue with a group of fifteen to twenty-five participants, this first stage may take all or most of the first session.

The second stage is similar in some ways to the creative block that an artist sometimes feels when facing a blank canvas, except that in this case, the group is facing walls, and these walls are *full* of chart paper with tons of things written on them. The group is now wondering, "How will we ever reconcile all this?"

While this stage is challenging, it is relatively brief. Of course, a minute or two can feel like a century when the facilitator's main job is to hold the creative tension and refrain from jumping in to steer the process. This second stage is *not* the equivalent of the "groan zone," the difficulty experienced in various processes that attempt to manage a group into convergence. Instead, in Dynamic Facilitation convergence and divergence emerge naturally as alternating phases of the creative flow. The Yuck Stage is a momentary and transitional state of being overwhelmed, experienced when first facing the full complexity of an issue.

The third stage usually begins when one of the participants, faced with all of the various perspectives gathered in the first stage and sitting in the charged silence of the transitional second stage, offers a new creative insight to the group. This typically sparks other participants' contributions, and the group begins operating at a different level. The facilitator continues recording individual contributions, just as in the first stage. Yet some things are different: the energy has shifted, and the ideas being offered are new, informed by the shared map that the group has created. Often the facilitator is able to fade into the background while continuing to record participants' contributions. However, he or she remains alert in case there is a need to step in and create space for apparently conflicting perspectives by listening fully to each participant, as in the first stage.

The fourth stage usually begins when there is a clear call for action by a participant. Someone wants to know how this admittedly helpful big picture that has been generated is going to be concretized into actionable steps. At this point, a second level of purging helps participants shift into their commitments for action.

Once a group is in a flow state, there is often a natural oscillation between the third and the fourth stages. A group may reach the point of generating some concrete action plans regarding a specific topic and then shift naturally into a big-picture conversation about yet another challenge.

Helping Groups through the Yuck

After the initial Purging Stage of a meeting, we find that there is generally a critical transition stage. The facilitator has already drawn forth the various perspectives present in the group, the walls are covered with chart paper, and the participants are often feeling somewhat overwhelmed by the divergence they are facing. While this stage usually only lasts a few minutes, those few minutes can feel quite long!

At this point, we might use the following interventions:

Waiting—being comfortable with the silence and with not knowing. This can be harder than it sounds, as a minute of silence can feel like an eternity.

Recapping—if needed, and then shifting back into silence. For example, I might say something like: "Well, it seems from the charts that some of you feel strongly one way, while others have a very different perspective…and then here are some additional points that have been raised."

Resisting—we need to resist the temptation to jump in and rescue the group. (Back to number one above—time to wait some more!)

At some point during this brief but challenging phase, someone in the group will inevitably come up with a creative inspiration. "Wait! I just had a thought! What if we…" This spark, in turn, will evoke additional solutions, concerns, and questions from the rest of the group, and then the group will be off and running again.

While the process the facilitator uses remains the same—charting people's ideas, perspectives, inquiries, and concerns on the various charts—the quality of the group's thinking tends to be fresher and more inclusive at this stage. The solutions that participants propose are no longer the ones that they walked in with. In general, people are attempting to respond to the diversity of perspectives that has emerged in the first phase.

Most significantly, the facilitator does not *take any of the suggested proposals and attempt to lead the group into a negotiated process so that they can all "decide" upon a solution.* Instead, he or she continues recording the flow of the choice-creating conversation. However, in this third stage, the facilitator often finds that he or she can recede into more of a background role while remaining alert, being on call as needed.

Remaining in a Creative Flow

In our experience, the flow of divergence—convergence, divergence, convergence, etc.—happens quite spontaneously when a group is in a creative flow. Therefore, once the facilitator has helped a group enter a creative zone, the task becomes to help them remain in it.

The facilitator does this by continuing to listen deeply and record the flow of conversation. In this third stage, since participants have usually become more comfortable sharing their ideas and concerns, the facilitator will usually not need to work as hard to draw them out. Also, since participants have begun to listen to one another more deeply and express curiosity about any divergences that emerge, the facilitator can often take more of a background role.

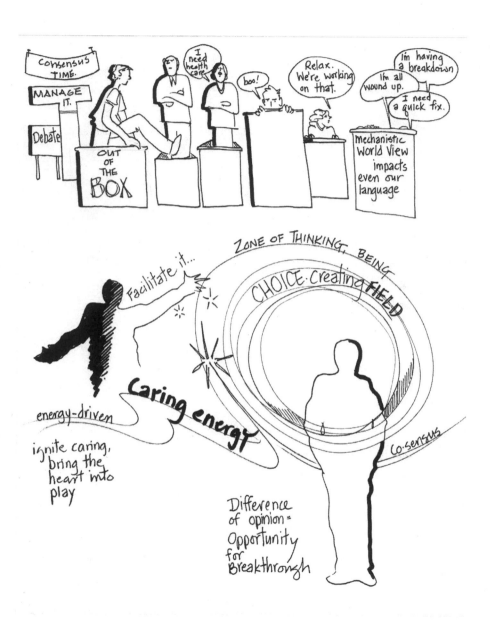

Helping a group remain in a creative process…

However, it is vital that the facilitator continue following the conversation very closely and jump in when needed to create space for divergence, especially whenever it seems that people may begin to become polarized around apparently contradictory ideas.

It is key for the facilitator to help the group remain in a creative process by refraining from any attempt to manage toward agreement or consensus. This generally includes refraining from voting, show of hands, or any other forms of agree-or-disagree thinking conventionally used in the struggle to arrive at formal decisions. Of course, there are some situations where for informational purposes, we may want to know what the majority of people are feeling in a given situation. But with choice-creating, we are not looking for a majority opinion to reach convergence. We are also *not* looking to nudge people closer to the majority opinion, in order to "create consensus." Instead, *we are actively seeking the kind of synthesis and breakthrough that can occur from listening deeply to the "weak signals" of the* minority *perspectives.*

Most of us have learned to define agreement as that which ensues after a formal decision-making process. Therefore, refraining from formal agreement is one of the ways in which Dynamic Facilitation differs most profoundly from conventional facilitation. At the same time, we do not want to promote any false consensus or groupthink. Therefore, instead of attempting to negotiate consensus before it happens, we take time to carefully explore with the group any *apparent* shared understandings, convergences, or breakthroughs that seem to have emerged. We do so retroactively—*after* they have already appeared.

In a creative process, any convergences that the group reaches, whether real or apparent, will quite quickly open up to the next level of divergence. We do not call attention to convergence in the moment, but wait until after the group has begun working on a new level of divergence. Then we check in to see whether everyone is really on board, and create space for any groupthink tendencies to dissolve. We will continue to discuss how this is done, with a real-life example. But first, we will be looking at the spontaneous flow of divergence-convergence-divergence.

Each Arrival as a New Point of Departure

As an example of what an ongoing flow of divergence-convergence-divergence might look like, let us take a very prosaic example from daily life. Imagine for a moment a middle-class family planning to go on vacation. At the beginning of the conversation, each person is starting out with a different idea of where he or she wants to go. Everyone talks for a while about their particular preferences and then some new ideas begin to arise, as family members begin to attempt to include the preferences of each person. At some point, the teenage son mentions that he has heard about a dude ranch out west. If the family goes there, Sis will get to go horseback riding, Mom and Dad will get to camp, and he can sit around the campfire practicing his guitar.

It is apparent that everyone is excited about this new idea, and then Mom brings up the question of how to get there. She has always wanted to ride a train, but it will take an extra three days to get there that way. Dad mentions that if the family drives, they could visit Uncle Bob along the way. Meanwhile, Sis has been accumulating frequent flyer miles, and she prefers to fly.

It is obvious that once the destination is determined, there is a whole new set of issues that arise. Furthermore, once the transportation issue is figured out, the family will be faced with a whole new set of tasks, which might include what to take on the trip, what kind of arrangements to make to take care of the house in the family's absence, etc. In fact, from a pessimistic perspective, we could say that every convergence or agreement about what to do just opens up a whole new set of divergences. At the same time, the group is in fact making progress!

In the absence of a conventional agree-disagree process, the group can easily miss that *they are now working on a whole new set of challenges, having already solved the original issues they were facing at the beginning of the meeting.* In fact, this often happens. Taking a moment to stop and verify the convergences provides an additional opportunity to pause and help the group acknowledge the progress it has made.

Let's apply this to the above example. A few minutes into the conversation about modes of transportation, someone taking on the role of facilitator might say: "Well, when we started, we were trying to figure out where to go for our vacation. Now it seems we are all happy with the idea of going to a dude ranch" (taking a minute to look around for nods). "And so now we seem to be at the next step: figuring out how we will get there. It appears that there are a number of different ideas on the table, so if we're all on board, let's continue to think creatively about this."

Disconfirming the Appearance of Convergence

What if, in the example we just gave, something different happens when we attempt to verify that everyone *is* indeed happy with the idea of going to the dude ranch? What if Sis were to say, "Well..." and then look down?

From a Dynamic Facilitation perspective, it would be clear that we had not, in fact, fully purged everyone. When we check an apparent convergence, at first we may find that one or more participants have been holding back thoughts and feelings, hesitating about the appropriate time to share them.

No problem! We know what to do. The facilitator needs to genuinely welcome this as an opportunity to listen deeply to the person who, up to now, has been holding back concerns. After fully listening to that person's concerns, alternative solutions, and/or alternative problem statements, the facilitator then continues to listen to whatever arises next, helping the group remain in a creative flow. By doing so, it is much more likely that the next time the group arrives at a point of convergence, it will be something that everyone is truly excited about.

As we circle back to listen deeply to someone who is *not* fully comfortable with what appeared to be a convergence, we are letting each participant know that each individual voice and perspective is important. Participants begin to realize that their full participation is needed in order for the group to move forward.

What we do *not* want to do is jump on convergences just as they are beginning to emerge. We might be tempted to ask the group to vote or have a show of thumbs to make sure that they are all in agreement before allowing them to proceed to the next set of problems. Yet if we do so, we will only short-circuit the creative process and shortchange the group.

When we ask people to enter into agree-disagree thinking, we are stepping out of the creative flow and re-entering the arena of bargaining, limited options, and power struggles. It is much better to wait a few minutes until the group appears to have experienced a shared shift, and then verify that everyone is in fact okay with the direction the group is going. If someone is not, this gives that person the opportunity to let you know. If, however, everyone is on board, the group members may simply look at you as if you have just asked a very obvious question and continue merrily along in their creative flow.

Choice Creating as an Alternative to Decision Making

What if, in the above example, we are not meeting around a kitchen table talking about a family vacation but, instead, at a board meeting, creating an organizational plan? For a long time, I hesitated to offer Dynamic Facilitation as an alternative to conventional decision-making processes. The reason for this is exemplified in a story that Jim Rough tells about a meeting he facilitated that appeared in many ways to have been quite successful. Afterward, one of the participants approached Jim in obvious distress. He demanded, "When did we decide on this?" pointing to the items on the Outcomes Chart.

One (not very helpful) answer might have been, "Well, that's what this whole meeting has been about!" Instead, Jim gently asked the participant if he had any concerns or objections to any of the items on the Outcomes Chart. The participant shook his head; no he did *not* have any objections to any of the items. In fact, he *wanted* the results on that page, but he was uncomfortable with not having used the normal decision-making process. There was no familiar sequence of steps to signal how it was that these items had been decided upon.

Until recently, my own solution to this challenge was to offer Dynamic Facilitation as a purely exploratory process, designed to build shared systemic understanding, enhance creativity, and generate new choices while leaving any formal decision making to whatever conventional process a group was already using. Yet this is not always so practical, and the reality is that shared outcomes—whether "ahas," "of courses," or "clear next steps forward"—do in fact emerge in our work, often "evaporating" the need for making a subsequent decision with regard to that issue.

Recently I discovered a simple step that affords me greater ease in offering Dynamic Facilitation as an alternative approach to conventional decision making. In fact, it is so simple, that it seems obvious in hindsight. These days, whenever I stop to retroactively check on an apparent convergence (as described in the previous section), I add one small step. If everyone appears to be on the same page, rather than allowing them to move on after five to ten seconds, *I invite participants to take forty seconds in silence to check in and see whether they are fully comfortable moving forward with this apparent convergence.* Taking this time makes it very clear when and how we "made the decision" to do X or Y.

It's still important to do this retroactively, only after sensing that a shift may have already taken place. And of course, any concerns that may emerge after the long pause are fully welcomed and heard. I have found that invariably, they help to improve the final outcome.

A Meeting of Minds and Hearts

Hopefully, it is becoming clear that when we speak of convergence in Dynamic Facilitation, we are not speaking about the kind of formal decisions that groups usually struggle to make, within some constrained view of the problem. Instead, we are talking about "felt shifts" in participants' energy, attention, and focus, which we verify after the fact. This verifying process is an opportunity to make sure that all of the divergence present in the group is being brought to the surface and to welcome any voices that have not yet emerged.

On one occasion, a colleague and I were working with the sales and warehouse departments of a winery in Sonoma County. As part of

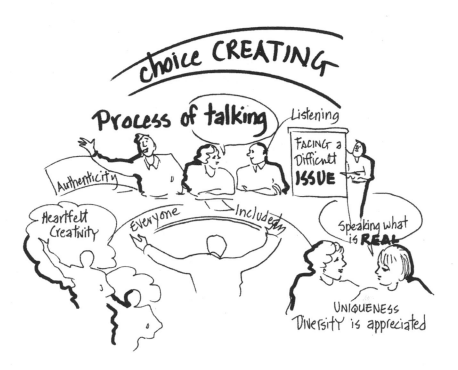

Remaining in a creative process results in...

a longer session, we spent about forty-five minutes using Dynamic Facilitation to explore a problem that the company was experiencing with deliveries. Truckers were showing up extremely late for their pick-up appointments, to the great exasperation and considerable inconvenience of the warehouse staff. The group explored a variety of possible responses to the problem. When the solution at last emerged, it seemed clear to the whole group that the problem had been solved and there was no need to discuss it further (Zubizarreta, 2013).

Afterward, we debriefed the session. One of the participants began to say that he particularly appreciated how the group had "come to a consensus," but stopped himself in mid-sentence. Instead, he paused for a second, and then said, "...arrived at a meeting of the minds."

Although I had not explained very much about the process, this participant clearly sensed that we had *not* struggled to reach a decision in the usual way that consensus is often negotiated. Instead, something else had happened: we had reached a meeting of the minds—and of the hearts as well. We call this kind of powerful convergence a breakthrough. This is what Dynamic Facilitation is designed to evoke.

Sometimes breakthroughs arrive in the form of a new problem statement, around which the whole group coalesces, instead of a solution. In a seminar group exploring the abortion issue, the breakthrough came in the form of a shared inquiry. Instead of "What should we do about abortion?" or any of the other problem statements that had emerged in the process of that conversation, the group discovered that the real problem statement around which they had all converged was, "How do we create a world where every child is a wanted child?" Of course, that creative challenge generated a whole new set of solutions, concerns, problem statements, etc., but it was a challenge that everyone was excited to work on.

Still other times, the breakthrough may not be either a new solution or a new problem-statement, but rather a new sense of the situation itself. Or it may be a newfound sense of empowerment or wholeness within the group. There is a tremendous amount of energy that is generated when people realize that others also care and want to contribute. The differences in perspective that had led to friction, tension, and conflict become much more comprehensible as we develop a shared understanding of the larger system, and each person's unique role within it.

Letting Go and Allowing

There is a degree of paradox at the heart of Dynamic Facilitation. To allow breakthroughs to happen, we need to release our attachment to having breakthroughs. If we are too invested in the outcome, we try to control or direct the process in some fashion, which makes it less likely for a breakthrough to emerge. Instead, when we are willing to risk, trust, and let go of control, we create the conditions that allow breakthroughs to take

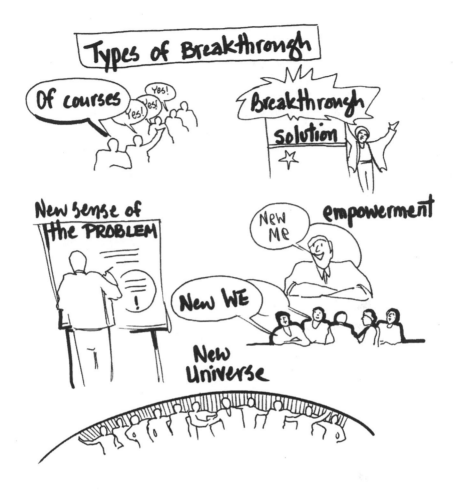

place—in their own time and manner.

Yet our trust in the process is not blind trust. Instead, it is based on our experience. A key element of the seminars consists of providing participants with enough experience in self-organizing groups to trust the process enough to apply it. As they do so, practitioners gain more experience, thus deepening their trust in this work and in groups' potential for self-organization.

Another paradoxical aspect has to do with the relationship between individual and group. In Dynamic Facilitation, we are fiercely protective of participants' individuality, never seeking to persuade people to modify their position for the presumed good of the group. Yet it is this same emphasis on continually making room for individual creativity that allows powerful group breakthroughs to occur: "When every 'I' is heard, a 'we' can form."

This paradox is not new. For example, in diversity work, participants often experience a much deeper sense of unity as a result of making room for each person's unique history and identities. However, we are not accustomed to applying this insight to the realm of generating practical group outcomes. Instead, there is a strong belief that we must bargain or negotiate in order to achieve any common agreement, or at least make an attempt to consciously distance ourselves somewhat from our individual positions. (This latter strategy can indeed be useful in situations when there is no facilitator available.)

In Dynamic Facilitation, we instead continually seek to elicit the fullness of individual creativity and diversity. We know that this fullness creates the rich ground for "co-sensing" as the group begins to develop a shared sense of the larger picture in all of its complexity. We know, too, that evolution happens at the fringes. *Whenever something occurs that we later realize was a convergence or a breakthrough, it begins as an individual contribution.* The person who is offering that particular contribution may not even feel particularly confident at the time that he or she will be understood. Sometimes a participant may be aware of saying something that will be of value to the group, but at other times, he or she may feel out in left field. In either case, we recognize it as a convergence to the extent that, after the fact, the whole group has moved forward and is able to recognize itself and its situation more clearly by means of that contribution.

From Shared Understanding to Action

When a group is engaged in a broad exploration of issues that matter and a greater shared understanding has begun to emerge, there is a natural point at which someone will put out a call for action. Often this is expressed by a participant saying something like, "Well, this larger exploration is all well and good, but what I want to know is what we're going to do tomorrow!"

There is a real risk here that the conversation can begin to shift back into what Jim Rough calls a transactional mode (win-lose, agree-disagree, detached, purely rational mode). If we want to help the group stay in a choice-creating process, our questions at this crucial juncture should serve to help keep the conversation in transformational mode (creative, authentic, involved, whole-person mode). We do this in a similar way to the way we began: *by inviting a purge.*

Chances are good that the person who is posing the moving-to-action problem statement ("How can we move from larger systemic understandings to practical outcomes?") *already* has an initial solution in mind. However, our first attempts may not succeed in drawing this out. The response to, "Well, if it were up to you, what might the action plan look like?" is likely to be a demurral: "Well, I would form a committee" or else, "I would have us all spend forty minutes talking about different options in order to consider various possibilities, and then create an action plan."

This kind of response is understandable from at least two perspectives. From the perspective of safety: people are naturally concerned about being seen as overbearing or as attempting to impose their will on others. We can create additional safety by posing the follow-up question in a hypothetical mode: "Okay, so let's imagine that we formed a committee and *then*, after the committee met and did all of their work, they came up with an action plan that made a lot of sense to you. What might it look like?"

This kind of question will often elicit a laugh, followed by a greater risk-taking response, as the person opens up and shares what his or her own ideal action plan would look like. Of course, as facilitators, we write this down as a possible solution, mirroring it back to check for understanding. At this point it is particularly important to encourage the participant to be as specific as possible: so for instance, if someone were to say, "I'd have three people draft a new ordinance by Friday," I would ask who those three people would be and whether it would be Friday morning, noon, or end of day, and what the ordinance would say.

Once the participant has fully sketched out the action plan (usually finishing with, "But of course that's only my idea, I don't know what other people would think…") we continue as we have been, opening the floor to any concerns, alternative solutions from others, etc.

Here is where the surprise is likely to happen. Assuming that the group has been engaging in an authentic exploration of the larger issues, it is quite likely that the participant will look around the table and realize that others are in full or nearly full agreement with his or her proposed action plan, often having only minor modifications to suggest. Why does this happen so frequently? It seems to be the result of the large degree of shared systemic understanding that has already been created through the open-ended, creative process in which we have been field-testing initial solutions all along.

From the perspective of past experience, there is a second understandable reason for the initial demurral to offer a solution at this stage. People tend to assume that coming up with an action plan *must* be a long and tedious process, simply because that is how it's been in the past. Yet, when we engage in a different approach, participants discover it really doesn't need to be that way.

Of course, the initial person who asked for an action plan was likely to be focusing on only some of the things that need to be done. Other people will likely follow suit by bringing up other requests for action on other aspects of the issue. Even though the group has just experienced a successful bid for action, it's often the case that the next participants to call for action will also need some additional help and encouragement to share *their own* solutions for the specific action needs they are perceiving.

As facilitators, we are clearly not pressing for convergence at this point, just as we have not done so at any other point. If it turns out that someone in the group *does* have an issue with a proposed action plan, or with a part of one, then that becomes a concern that is fully heard and mirrored back. The owner of the concern is asked if there might be a different preferred solution that he or she would be willing to put forth. Or maybe this participant realizes that there is another issue altogether that needs to be addressed before finalizing the prior action plan.

The principle continues to be to bring the diversity of perspectives in the room to the surface, offer a full hearing to each, reflect back what we are hearing and seeing, and trust that the group will find its own "right next steps" as a result of this process.

CHAPTER SEVEN

Concluding Stages and Follow-up

Closing Stages of a Session

Since we are working with an emergent flow of divergence-convergence-divergence, etc., there are no guarantees that our meetings will end nicely right when we are at a major convergence point. In fact, that is not likely to happen. As we draw near the end of a meeting, the group may have experienced several convergences already and be in the middle of exploring a whole new set of challenges. Alternatively, if it is the first meeting on a large and complex issue, the group might still be in the midst of the initial Purge Stage and may not have reached any major convergences.

When a group has had a sufficiently large breakthrough in the middle of a meeting, they may not want or need to continue working on the next level of challenges right away. In this case, we may want to heed one of the laws of Open Space: "When it's over, it's over" (Owen, 1992). Even if we are only halfway through the allotted time, it may be a good time to end the meeting so the participants can begin to implement some of their discoveries.

At other times, we may want to use the time for shifting gears into a conversation about process, and what the group has learned from engaging in this creative approach. Or, a group may be so energized by a major breakthrough that they want to keep on going and begin working on their next challenging situation.

In any case, the facilitator needs to let the group know when the allotted time to end the meeting is approaching. This is especially important when participants have expressed a need to have a solution or outcome by the end of the meeting and they have not arrived at any convergences yet. Being aware of the approaching timeline sometimes helps participants shift naturally into a higher creative gear, and a breakthrough solution might emerge in the last few minutes of a meeting. However, this is not something that we can count on. Therefore, it is helpful to have explored both desired outcomes *and* default plans beforehand.

In addition, it is important to reserve some time at the end of the meeting to review the charts with the group, mark and celebrate their accomplishments, engage in a Content Closure, and also include Process Closure.

Creating Content Closure

When it is time to end the meeting, we need to help the group experience closure. There are a number of different ways that we might do so. Regardless of the way we choose, our larger purpose is threefold:

- Acknowledge the progress the group has made
- Summarize the current state of the conversation
- Create a marker to help the group start up their next session

Bookmark or Summary Outline This can be a useful way to track the progress that has been made, especially if the group is still in the initial Purging Stage (which is typical at the end of the first session). It's likely that there have not been any major breakthroughs yet, nor any action plans to put on the Outcomes Chart. Participants may have covered a great deal of ground yet feel overwhelmed that they are all over the map. Thus, it can be very helpful to close by creating a Bookmark or Summary Outline.

To do so, we ask participants for help in summarizing the larger flow of the conversation. What main themes were explored during the session? What is the current landscape now, including any unresolved divergences or polarities? It can be helpful to spend a few minutes reviewing all of the charts that have been created during the session as a way to harvest some summary statements.

As a graphic aid to the summarizing process, the facilitator can draw three boxes (three large rectangles) on a piece of chart paper and then ask, "If you had to come up with three statements that summarized some of the main points we explored today, what might they be? What should we write inside each of these boxes?"

Especially when the group is in the middle of a significant divergence, it is useful for the facilitator to help the group acknowledge all of the work that has been accomplished toward obtaining a fuller picture of the situation.

Please note that a summary statement does not have to imply agreement: for example, one very useful summary statement might be, "We are currently divided on the issue of X. Some of us feel strongly that A is the right course of action, while others of us feel strongly that B is the best way, and we are still in the middle of exploring each of these perspectives."

As participants propose various summary statements, sometimes two different statements might end up being combined, or one statement may be a subset or an example of another broader statement. Also, it's perfectly okay to end up with four or five summary statements instead of three; the initial number simply serves to jump-start the process.

When we complete the summary, the group is usually both surprised and relieved to see that all of the territory they have explored can be understood as examples or further details of the basic organizing skeleton they have just created in the form of a Bookmark or Summary Outline.

Creating a Group Symbol Alternatively, the facilitator might ask participants if someone would like to come up with a symbol that represents the current state of the conversation. If so, that person can be invited to come up and draw the symbol. Whether composed of words, symbols, or a combination of both, this Bookmark becomes a useful way to open the group's next meeting.

Creating a Group Story If the facilitator has the opportunity for some reflection time during a break in the meeting, this offers another possibility for content closure. The facilitator can review the charts to create a brief story or narrative that reflects the movement of the meeting. This story may include where the group started and the directions the conversation took, including any major shifts, and where the group seems to be at present.

The facilitator offers this story to the group, as a group-level reflection of the group's content exploration to date. As with any reflection, this story is offered to the group tentatively, as a prompt for their response and elaboration.

Outcomes Chart Another way to create content closure is by reviewing the charts with the group and pulling out any significant breakthroughs, convergences, "ahas," or "of courses" that the group has experienced onto a new Outcomes Chart.

This kind of closure is more likely if the group has had sufficient time to explore an issue and has thus naturally arrived at the point in the process where some convergences have actually occurred. For example, in a four-session process, we would be more likely to use this in the last three sessions.

In order to prepare for closure ahead of time, we can take some time during a break to highlight the various statements that have ended up being major turning points or convergences in the conversation. In this way, they will be easier to locate when it is time to create an Outcomes Chart.

In addition to major convergences or shared insights, the Outcomes Chart also includes any action commitments that individuals have made. For more on action planning, see pages 72-75.

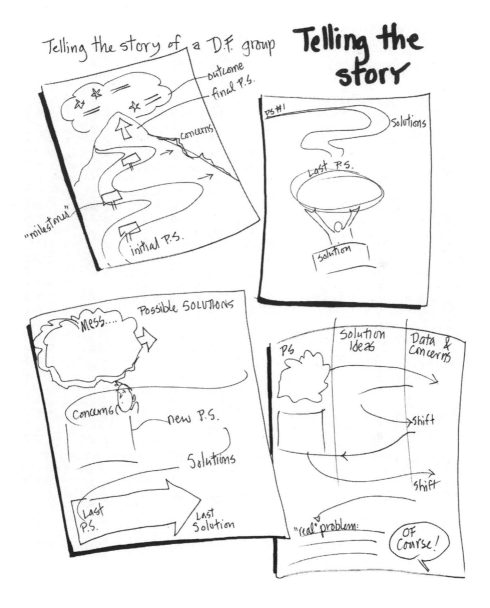

These templates can be used to tell the story
of a session or a series of sessions.

Creating Process Closure

Edward DeBono was one of the first to write about how any creative breakthrough will seem perfectly logical in hindsight. This is reflected in the name that we have given a certain kind of breakthrough that is typical in the DF process: the "of courses" that seem not just logical but also completely obvious *after* they have emerged into the group's consciousness.

At the same time, our experience has been that various kinds of breakthroughs that tend to emerge in a DF process are not just random luck, but are instead fairly reliable occurrences. We cannot predict exactly when in a group's process they will occur, nor what the content of the breakthrough will be; however, we are quite willing to guarantee that when certain basic conditions are present, these kinds of breakthroughs can and will occur.

It therefore feels important to leave some time at the end for group members to reflect on their experience of the process itself, so that they can develop a greater awareness of these basic conditions. This is a basic aspect of capacity building.

You may be familiar with a famous saying from the *Tao Te Ching*: "The mark of a great leader is that the people will say, 'We did it ourselves.'" We can easily substitute "facilitator" for "leader" here. Yet a drawback of having the leadership or facilitation function remain too invisible is that others may not learn how to fill that role. Sustainability implies building everyone's capacity to fulfill that invisible-yet-much-needed function.

Since the facilitator role in DF is quite non-directive in some ways, and the non-linear conversational flow of DF approximates natural conversation, in the absence of reflection it can be fairly common for group participants to attribute the success of a meeting to luck or happenstance. This can be followed by disappointment when, without anyone holding the space of designated listener/creativity evoker/creativity protector in their next meeting, old patterns tend to reappear.

In a culture that emphasizes short-term gain, it's understandable for a group that is delighted by what they have accomplished to be completely focused on how they can implement their new breakthrough while having little time or interest in pausing to reflect on how to build their capacity for future challenges. And so it can often feel somewhat jarring when we invite a group to pause and shift gears and reflect on the *process* rather than to continue working animatedly on the content as they have been doing up until this moment.

This can be reminiscent of the Yuck Stage we described earlier…a minute or two of interminable silence as the group shifts gears. Nonetheless, I have learned over time that it is essential to build in some reflection time at the end of sessions. This is where we invite participants to comment on their experience of the facilitated conversation—not the content, but the *way* in which the conversation was held—and what was distinctive or challenging or useful about it.

This reflection time is what we are calling the process closure. Just as at the beginning of an engagement, we introduce people to how we will be working together, at the end of an engagement we invite people to reflect on their experience of working together in this way. If we are doing a typical series of four dynamically facilitated sessions, we might have a briefer process closure at the end of each session, while saving time for a more in-depth process closure at the end of the fourth and last session in the series.

For briefer closure, we can use a "check-out circle" format where each person briefly shares their experience of the meeting. For example, we can ask participants to share a highlight or two of the session, or to state what it is that they are taking away from the meeting. For a more in-depth closure, we can invite some conversation about the process first, before concluding with a "check-out circle."

While we are primarily focused on group closure here, this may be a good place to mention the value of continuing to check in with the key meeting sponsors after each meeting. Just as we worked intensively with these organizational leaders beforehand, it is crucial to continue offering leaders one-on-one support, and to build in enough time to have individual closure with them as well. This creates a greater likelihood that the work the group is doing will be received and well-integrated into the functioning of the larger organization.

In many cases, a series of DF sessions will serve as a worthwhile creative interlude before participants return to "business as usual." However, it will have given them an opportunity to generate some in-depth shared understandings, come up with some significant breakthroughs, and experience a real taste of the power of co-intelligence and co-creativity. In order to ensure lasting benefits, it needs to become an ongoing practice, and part of an organization's DNA.

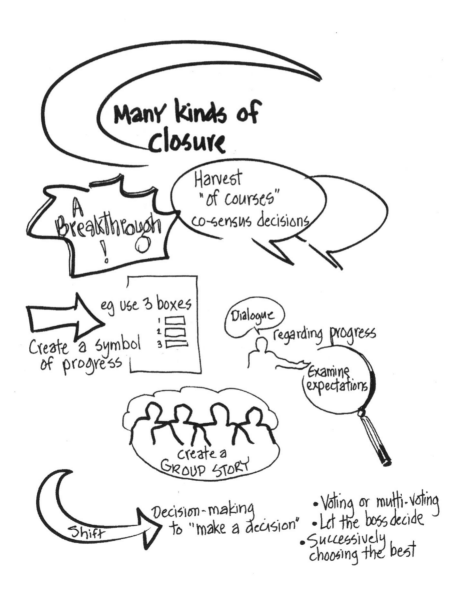

Harvesting the Charts after Each Session

The Problem-Statements, Solutions, Concerns, and Data Charts that have been created during the course of a DF meeting constitute a useful record of the group's creative journey. Even when a group has already arrived at their desired outcomes, the record of how they arrived there contains a wealth of information. It can serve as a rich source of questions for ongoing inquiry and a storehouse of creative ideas and information for later review.

The notes from the meeting also have a more immediate use. Experiencing the full scope of the Dynamic Facilitation process generally takes a series of three or four meetings. Transcribing the charts and creating a written document to share with the group before or at the beginning of the next meeting is a key part of the process. In addition to the benefits mentioned above, the meeting notes allow both facilitators and participants to stand back from the conversation enough to perceive its larger flow and coherence in a way that we are often unable to notice when in the thick of things.

Transcribing the charts is usually much less tedious than it sounds. Facilitators often experience a sense of reliving the meeting as they transcribe the notes. This can help the facilitator reconstitute the original statements. For the sake of readability, he or she may choose to expand the notes somewhat from the abbreviated manner in which they may have originally been recorded. Of course it is important that the meaning not be altered in the process.

Since long lists of any kind are hard to read, it makes sense to "chunk" the material for ease of presentation. For example, we might group together a set of four items and then add an extra blank line between one group of items and the next. In addition, the facilitator may choose to add some retroactive organization by simply regrouping similar items together and adding subheaders. This is similar to the data crunch in Action Research methodology: all of the original data is retained while being lightly sorted and clustered for meaning.

It is a hallmark of the creative process that, in hindsight, the results appear perfectly linear and logical. (Edward de Bono explains this brilliantly in *Serious Creativity*, 1992.) While the process of Dynamic Facilitation might feel somewhat unpredictable at times, often the greatest surprise is the natural order and practical clarity of the results that we obtain, in addition to how much ground a group has been able to cover.

Following up with Action Plans and More

When a group has created action items as part of the outcomes of a meeting, it makes sense to start the subsequent meeting with a review of those action plans. However, it is key that, as facilitators, our goal is to facilitate learning, not to serve as de facto project manager.

When following up with action items, the most helpful stance from a facilitation perspective is one of interested curiosity. What have we learned? This same question holds regardless of whether the action plan was fulfilled or not. If we did carry out our stated intentions, what did we learn by doing so? Or, if we did not carry out the action item as planned, what can we learn by looking at what happened instead?

This stance supports the group by offering continuity—we do not ignore what has come before, including our earlier intentions and commitments. At the same time, we leave the door open for learning, change, and growth. It may be the case that the original action plan was too ambitious or did not take some crucial factors into account. Or, some unexpected circumstances arose that altered the whole situation. It is not our role to hold anyone accountable; we are simply exploring what happened so we can all take in and process the information. In turn, this prepares us to explore where we are now and where we need to go in the current session.

This attitude of discovery is especially relevant when we are following up with past solution ideas that did *not* become action items. The value of doing so is something I stumbled across by accident when working with a cross-departmental group in a local hospital. By the beginning of our fourth session together, the participants in the group had already accomplished a great deal of what they had initially set out to do.

At the beginning of our fourth session, it seemed that participants were much less engaged than they had been until that point. All of the action items from the third session had been accomplished, and so I briefly considered applying the Open Space law of "When it's over, it's over" and cancelling the meeting. However, it had taken so much effort to find times when we could all meet that I hesitated to do so. Instead, it occurred to me that it might be worth exploring how participants might be feeling at present about all of the other solution ideas that had been generated during the highly productive second and third sessions. The large majority of these ideas had not evoked sufficient whole-group momentum to become action items, but they had still been recorded in the notes.

And so I invited participants to go through the notes with me. I mentioned that it was possible that in the time since we had last met, they might have come across more information or new perspectives. This might lead them to now discard some of those initial solution ideas, instead of leaving them in a bin marked "maybe someday." Alternatively, they might now realize that a given idea really would be worth following up on at some future point. I was curious to see how they were presently holding these various creative possibilities generated in the two earlier sessions.

To everyone's surprise, including my own, it turned out that many of the solution ideas on the list had inspired individual participants to begin useful experiments within their own realms of individual and departmental authority. More surprising still, they had not been aware of one another's experiments until this moment.

As participants continued to share their findings, the energy in the room picked up, and the group began to explore a new level of challenges. I finished going through the list of earlier solutions with them, and then we shifted naturally back into regular DF mode. As it turned out, there were plenty of additional challenges that they wanted to talk about. By the end of the session, they had spontaneously identified the next organizational area that would need attention and who would need to be present in the room in order to work on it.

From this experience, I learned how any method that encourages a creative self-organizing process to take place will generate more results than are easily visible. If we want to harvest those results, we need to be intentional about it. We can create an opportunity to inquire about the various individual initiatives that participants have been experimenting with—over and beyond the explicit action items that came out of the meeting.

When we do this, it provides us with some useful information about the effects of the work we have done together. At the same time, it offers participants an opportunity to share their self-initiated learnings and update one another with their findings. In some situations, we may want to intentionally build in a fifth meeting for doing this kind of review, some three to six months after we have concluded a four-session sequence with a group.

It may seem obvious, but it may be worth stating that a single series of four sessions is not enough to embed this self-organizing approach to working with challenging issues into the ongoing culture of an organization. However, it can be a good starting point for developing a sense of what is possible with regard to establishing a culture of creativity and innovation.

CHAPTER EIGHT

Applying Dynamic Facilitation

When Is Dynamic Facilitation Appropriate?
Dynamic Facilitation is a powerful and effective approach for practical problem solving as well as for addressing difficult social issues. Below are some considerations to keep in mind as you apply this approach in a variety of situations.

Groups Facing Practical Issues Facilitators have used this approach to evoke outstanding outcomes in a wide variety of practical contexts, such as strategic planning, process improvement, and team-building. When applied skillfully, results include breakthrough solutions in formerly "stuck" situations, high-energy follow-through, shared systemic ("big picture") understandings, and better interpersonal relationships.

Dynamic Facilitation is especially useful when:

- a group is facing a complex situation

- there are no easy answers
- there is a lot of divergence, tension, and/or conflict

There are other situations in which Dynamic Facilitation may be *less* useful or when we need to take into account certain other considerations:

Caution: When a group needs to make a decision quickly Since Dynamic Facilitation helps participants develop a complex understanding of the "big picture" and evokes high levels of creativity, it may not seem to fit at first glance for a situation in which a group is in a hurry to arrive at a decision. However, even though this approach generally requires some time invested up front, it also tends to be much more efficient in the long run.

Decisions that are made on the basis of negotiated agreements can fall apart afterward, leading to difficulties in implementation. In contrast, the breakthroughs that emerge from a process where divergence is fully welcome tend to be more stable and are accompanied by high levels of commitment and energy. This can save much time in the implementation phase.

Even when there is not sufficient time available to allow convergences to emerge naturally, this approach can still be used for a shorter period of time as a support for creative exploration. At the end of that time, the group can return to their "fall-back" decision-making process. Even though it's unlikely that the group will have had enough time to arrive at any major breakthroughs, they will have gained a fuller understanding of the complexities inherent in the situation and may have even begun to think creatively about it.

Caution: When the choice is constrained to a fixed set of options Since Dynamic Facilitation excels at evoking creativity, it may not be a good fit in a situation where there is no room for thinking outside the box. However, a group might decide to spend a meeting thinking creatively anyway, even with the knowledge that at the end of the day, they will need to limit themselves to choosing from a constrained set of options. (It's always possible that, along the way, they will discover that there really are more options than they initially realized and come up with a way to implement the new choices they have created.)

Extreme caution: When the decision has already been made Like any other method, Dynamic Facilitation is *not* applicable for situations in which the only desired outcome is "buy-in" with regard to a decision that has already been made. Here is the shadow side of the practice of facilitation; too often facilitators are hired to give the illusion of participation rather than the substance. This is clearly unacceptable and unethical.

Yet, *there is a constructive and ethical way to work within a situation where a leader has already made a decision.* We do so by encouraging leaders to take responsibility for making the power dynamics of the situation explicit and aboveboard.

For example, a manager may be willing to participate in a group exploration to see whether a better option can be found than the one he or she has already decided upon. Jim Rough calls this the *"this, or something better…"* approach. The manager introduces the meeting by openly acknowledging that he or she has already arrived at a fallback decision, yet wants to engage in some exploratory field-testing before implementation. If the group (including the manager, who will be participating actively and authentically in the facilitated process) can arrive together at something that everyone (including the manager) sees as a better solution, then the manager will consider adopting that solution. Otherwise, the existing decision will stand.

If this approach is undertaken as a good-faith effort, the results are guaranteed to be win-win regardless of the particular outcome. Given enough time to arrive at a breakthrough, one possible outcome is that the group will indeed come up with a solution that is truly an improvement on the original one in the eyes of *everyone* present, including the manager. Alternatively, the group will rediscover the manager's original plan; however, now it is fully their own. As such, they are energized and motivated to implement it.

If there is *not* sufficient time for the group to reach a real break-through, the benefits may be limited to a greater understanding of the various perspectives present in the group, as well as a greater understanding of the strengths and limitations of the particular decision that the manager will be making. In this case, it may be that the disadvantages of using this method could outweigh the possible advantages, as stimulating people's creativity in a situation where there is no real opportunity for input could lead to greater frustration. In those circumstances—a decision has already been made, and there is too little time to engage in an authentic exploration of possible alternatives—it may be preferable to use a less creative method to ascertain group members' responses to the already-determined decision.

Dynamic Facilitation for Dialogue on Social Issues This approach can be especially useful for situations in which greater understanding among different groups is sought. People who have not experienced the process firsthand may be concerned about the focus on problem statements, solutions, and concerns, wondering how these can be compatible with dialogue, especially in situations where the purpose of dialogue is not to address practical situations but simply to increase understanding.

However, we know that nothing brings people together more quickly than working on a common problem. Framing an issue in terms of what can be done about it (*How might we find a way to…?*) and eliciting people's creativity in the form of solutions (*I think we could…*) helps create a sense of collaboration and shared purpose. We have found this to be highly effective even when a group is primarily focused on exploring an issue rather than taking action.

Of course, eliciting people's creativity in this way requires the facilitator to play an active role in protecting each person's contribution and making room for a diversity of perspectives, especially in situations of high conflict. Given the highly active role of the facilitator, this approach can be especially helpful for facilitating dialogue in situations where people may have different ways of communicating and be unwilling or unable to agree to many ground rules. It can also serve as a useful way to de-escalate a conflict that has already erupted. The facilitator's skill in welcoming and truly listening to each participant's contribution can help people feel genuinely heard. As a result, they can often begin to enter into a more creative and constructive conversation.

Working as a Facilitation Team

While it's possible to do Dynamic Facilitation as a single facilitator, many

of us find it preferable to work as part of a facilitation team. There are several advantages to doing so, including the opportunity to support our own learning process by having someone to debrief and reflect with afterward. Another benefit is having more people present to host the group. As the Art of Hosting folks like to say, "It takes a field to host a field."

When working as a facilitation team, we have additional support for tracking what is going on in the room. When we are listening to each person, reflecting, and recording their contributions, it can be hard to notice what else may be happening in the group. Of course, if we are working alone, we can ask the participants to help us keep track of who else may want to speak. Yet having a facilitation team, rather than a single facilitator, is ideal.

One thing we do *not* generally recommend, however, is having one person doing the listening while another person is doing the recording. People often ask about this, since it can feel daunting to listen *and* record at the same time. However, we have found that listening is a very personal phenomenon; what one person is hearing and reflecting back can be significantly different from what another person is hearing and recording. Of course, if you have experience working closely with another person, you might be able to find a way to work around this challenge.

Another benefit of having the same person listening, reflecting, and recording is that it allows us to slow down the pace of the group as needed. People often ask if it wouldn't be more efficient to have one person reflect and another record. Yet faster is not always more effective, especially when listening is concerned. There can be great value in the group having time to digest the contribution that someone has just made.

Instead of splitting up the listening/reflecting/writing role, we've found that it can be helpful to take turns being in that role. Team members who are not currently in the listening/writing/reflecting role can hold space, pay attention to what is happening in the group, help move the charts, etc. And, of course, one of the most delightful experiences is when everyone in the room is a trained Dynamic Facilitator and is able to take a turn facilitating as needed!

The Wisdom Council: A Microcosm That Affects the Larger Whole

The Wisdom Council is a particularly exciting way to apply Dynamic Facilitation to work with a larger system, such as an organization or community. The purpose of the Wisdom Council is to raise the quality of the conversation in the larger system. We do this by periodically bringing together a microcosm of the whole, designed to include a wide diversity of perspectives, to creatively address the issues that affect everyone in the system, and then feed their findings back to the whole.

To create a Wisdom Council process, the first step is to select the scope by defining the community of people who form the system we are addressing. Then, we:

- Gather together a microcosm of the community by means of random selection
- Invite this microcosm to participate in a two-day, dynamically facilitated "intensive." The only agenda to discuss is what each person sees as the most significant issues in their organization or community and what each person thinks should be done about them.
- Toward the end of their time together, help participants identify areas of common ground that have emerged, and thread those into a final outcome.
- At the conclusion of the two-day intensive, help participants share their story and their outcomes with a gathered assembly of the larger whole.
- Spark a broader conversation by inviting the community to reflect and dialogue about the findings of the Wisdom Council.
- Repeat this process periodically, convening a new, randomly selected microcosm quarterly, biannually, or annually.

With regard to the larger system, the outcomes of the Wisdom Council serve to bring deeper issues to a more conscious awareness in such a way that people in the larger system are able to engage with them constructively.

In part, this is because the group that is bringing these issues to light (the randomly selected constituents of the Wisdom Council) is a microcosm of the larger whole. Also key, this microcosm is not polarized, nor stuck in negativity. Instead, having been immersed in a choice-creating environment where each perspective is heard and valued, the Wisdom Council arrives at its conclusions full of creative energy and a sense of possibility.

So the message of the Wisdom Council is not just the recorded outcomes. As valuable as these outcomes can be for raising consciousness of issues that the system had previously not been grappling with adequately, the larger message is the experience of the Wisdom Council itself. We usually find that the people who are randomly selected to participate in the Wisdom Council are extremely moved by the experience. Having a two-day immersion in choice-creating conversation on the topic of the well-being of the system as a whole seems to reawaken participants' sense of agency, community, and possibility to a remarkable degree. During the reporting-out phase, offering participants the opportunity to share personal stories of their own experience of the Wisdom Council is a powerful complement to the group's recorded outcomes and findings.

Together, the stories and the findings of the Wisdom Council literally deepen the quality of the conversation throughout the system. For some people, this may not seem like much of a contribution; others will realize how significant and worthwhile an accomplishment this can be.

One pioneer in the use of Wisdom Councils within the corporate sector has been SwissCom, the Swiss telecommunications company. In the public sector, the success of this work in Vorarlberg, Austria, has inspired a growing number of local governments in Austria, Switzerland, and Germany to start exploring this work. They have renamed dynamically facilitated Wisdom Councils (and Creative Insight Councils, described below) as "BürgerInnen-Räte," and are finding them to be a particularly effective format for public engagement.

Another related large-group application of Dynamic Facilitation is to host an intensive with a microcosm group brought together to address a particular issue. These "Creative Insight Councils" differ from Wisdom Councils in having a pre-established topic. This format has also been very effective at evoking powerful perspectives and creative solutions as feedback for the larger whole.

There are, of course, more details to organizing and hosting a Wisdom Council or a Creative Insight Council than I have been able to include in this brief description. The main purpose here is to point to the existence of these formats, as well as to the value they can bring. If you are interested, I hope you will continue to explore further. If you contact Dynamic Facilitation Associates at www.DynamicFacilitation.com, we will be glad to put you in touch with others who have been experimenting in this area.

Using Dynamic Facilitation with One's Own Self or One-on-One

It can be particularly useful to apply Dynamic Facilitation as a framework to enhance our own personal growth and development. One example might be to use DF with a journaling practice to help when struggling with a challenging issue. To do so, we take a regular piece of lined paper, fold it into quarters, and begin jotting down a description of the challenge (data and problem statement), things we've already tried (initial solutions), why they didn't or won't work (concerns), feelings we are having about all this (more data), etc. Once we have all this down on paper, we can give ourselves some time to be with the whole of it, and see what comes next.

This framework can also be applied as a way to offer some helpful listening time to a friend or close person who may be struggling with a creative challenge. A note of caution: when working with someone we know, the biggest challenge can be resisting the temptation to fall into giving advice. We can make this easier by briefly describing the process to the person to whom we will be listening so they can remind us, as needed, to stay in our role.

As facilitators, our work is simply to listen, to check whether we have understood the various aspects of the situation by reflecting back the content and the feelings we are hearing, and to practice our recording skills by writing down those various aspects in the respective categories. We can also practice a few key invitations, such as "Tell me more," and "If you were to give yourself permission to consider anything at all, what would you really like to do to solve this situation?"

We can also practice making room for all of the different perspectives that might be voiced within the one person to whom we are listening. It is very common for all of us to have mixed feelings: a part of us wants to do something, yet another part of us has some concerns about it.

As we listen, it's helpful to notice the small yet significant shifts in perspective that happen in how the person is holding the situation. Sometimes our own expectations of facilitating a dramatic breakthrough can lead us to overlook that the person sitting in front of us has just come up with a new way of relating to the situation that feels quite different from where they originally started out!

Our one-on-one practice can be enhanced by learning other compatible methods that specialize in this kind of inner listening, such as Focusing and Inner Empathy work. In turn, anything that deepens our one-on-one listening skills will also enhance our Dynamic Facilitation work with groups.

What's Next? Continuing to Learn Dynamic Facilitation

In order to really learn Dynamic Facilitation, the best way is to find or create an opportunity to practice what you have read about in this manual. Below are some suggestions for how you might start doing so.

Experiment with Dynamic Facilitation on your own in connection with a group with whom you are already working. If you are already an experienced facilitator or a professional consultant, you will have many opportunities to experiment with this approach. I have tried to make this manual as complete as possible by offering all of the information that someone might need to carry out the process. I am delighted whenever I hear from people who have successfully experimented with the process, just from having read about it in the manual! At the same time, we have found that it often helps to have a learning community to deepen and extend one's learning. So we invite you to look at the Connecting with Other Practitioners of Dynamic Facilitation section below.

Attend an introductory seminar or workshop. Taking a hands-on seminar or workshop allows you to experience for yourself the unique power and flavor of this approach. I am one of a growing number of people who have been approved by Jim Rough to teach Dynamic Facilitation. You can find more information about my public workshops and my in-house workshops at www.DiaPraxis.com. I also offer individualized coaching for those wishing to learn this approach.

For additional learning opportunities throughout the globe, you can visit the Dynamic Facilitation Associates Web site at www.Dynamic-Facilitation.com.

For those of you who are active in the realm of social change, the Center for Wise Democracy offers partial scholarships to low-income activists and community organizers who want to learn Dynamic Facilitation. It is also possible to bring a seminar to your community if you have a number of people who are interested in attending. More information is available at www.WiseDemocracy.org.

Volunteer to facilitate a group. If you are a lay facilitator, you may want to gain experience by volunteering to facilitate a few sessions for a community group. It's helpful to give people a sense of what to expect ahead of time. When people hear the word "facilitation," they tend to assume that we are talking about a linear, control-oriented process instead of the creative exploration we have been describing here. So you may want to let people know that this approach is not "business as usual." Instead, it will help everyone develop a better understanding of the big picture and get on the same page. In turn, this usually leads to better practical outcomes.

Another way to create an opportunity to practice is to invite a group of friends over to your living room to participate in a creative exploration of challenging issues. We don't usually talk about issues such as politics or religion because they tend to be so divisive; however, when we use a creative process to safely explore our differences in these areas, we can end up with a better understanding of one another and a greater appreciation of how our differences bring value to the larger whole. If you share the process with your friends ahead of time, you can all work together to create a safe space. You may even want to take turns facilitating and become a practice group together.

Whether offering this work to a community group or a group of friends, it's helpful to frame it from the beginning as a larger process rather than just one meeting. People do not necessarily need to sign up for the whole thing up front; they may want to experience a taste first before making a longer commitment. By the end of the first session, participants will have had the opportunity to see for themselves to what extent each person is being heard, to what extent the conversation is focused on things that really matter, and to what extent they are learning something from the process. On this basis, they can decide whether or not they want to continue. At the same time, it's helpful to have created realistic expectations from the beginning by making it clear that some of the most significant fruits of the process, such as the sense of shared breakthroughs, will often take two or three sessions to develop.

Use the method individually or one-on-one. If you have not had much experience in working with groups, one good way to begin exploring this practice can be to use it with yourself or with another person in a one-on-one setting, as described earlier. Many of us who have been practicing Dynamic Facilitation for a long time continue to use it in this way, so this suggestion is not just for beginners. At the same time, it can be a good way to start!

Connect with other practitioners of Dynamic Facilitation. There is a great deal of informal support and mutual learning possible among people exploring Dynamic Facilitation who wish to deepen their skills. After a seminar, participants often stay in touch with one another and many find it helpful to form local practice groups.

The Center for Wise Democracy also maintains two e-mail list-servs, one for people who are interested in Dynamic Facilitation, and another one for people who are particularly interested in the Wisdom Council. You can sign up for these e-mail lists through the Web site of Dynamic Facilitation Associates at www.dynamicfacilitation.com.

ACKNOWLEDGMENTS

It has been a deep joy to write these words of acknowledgement, and to recognize how many people have contributed in various ways to this work. I realize that there are more of you than I am able to recall, and I apologize to anyone I may have unintentionally left out.

I want to begin by acknowledging the creative genius of Jim Rough and his passion for releasing the creative genius within all of us, both individually and collectively. Tom Atlee, mentor, friend, and colleague, introduced me to this work in 2000. Elliot Shuford, Win Stafford, and Tree Bressen were adventurous co-learners in that initial journey. Elliot and Win later assisted me in my first teaching efforts, for which I am extremely grateful. Tree has remained a continuous source of inspiration as a colleague and friend.

My initial experiences with Dynamic Facilitation confirmed my desire to learn more about groups and organizations. I was extremely fortunate to be a student of Saul Eisen, former director of the Organization

Development program at Sonoma State University. Heather Smith, professor of social psychology at SSU, directed my master's project on DF with great energy and enthusiasm. I am also deeply grateful to the practitioners who allowed me to interview them for that project.

Then there are the various clients who welcomed me into their organizations as a budding practitioner. I am especially grateful to Debbie Reno, Wendy Fantozzi, Sadhana Brent, Lisa Van de Water, Rick Phillips, Marcia Jo, and Dr. Joe Bujak, along with all of their various employees and co-workers.

When I created the first in-house edition of this DF manual, the enthusiastic feedback I received from Jeff Conklin, Al Selvin, and Simon Buckingham Shum was most affirming, especially since so much of what we do in this approach is counterintuitive to mainstream facilitation practice. (Of course, to practitioners of Dialogue Mapping, what we were doing seemed quite natural!) I am also grateful for Jack Travis' generous gift of professional editing services, which greatly improved the polish of that first version; to my mother, Alma Flor Ada, for her support in creating the Spanish version of this manual; and to Liliana Cosentino for her excellent translations.

During most of this last decade, Jean Rough (Jim's wife and partner) and DeAnna Martin have been dedicated co-explorers in this work, sharing experiences and reflecting together as we deepen our understandings. I am especially grateful for Jean's extensive support with the 2008 edition of the in-house manual, including her requests for new material on specific topics.

Ever since we met in 2002, Bruce Nayowith, my gifted and caring husband, has been contributing his own valuable insights and perspectives to this work. I am most grateful for his willingness to explore these principles in our daily life together, and the rich learning that continues to unfold from our ongoing conversations.

Extending my appreciation across the ocean, I also want to recognize some key players in the growth and development of this practice. In 2005, Matthias zur Bonsen, organizational consultant and author, invited Jim Rough to teach Dynamic Facilitation in Germany. Previously, Matthias had brought Marvin Weisbord and Sandra Janoff to teach Future Search, Harrison Owen to teach Open Space, and Birgitt Williams to teach Genuine Contact. Thus, he had developed a fertile network of consultants who were familiar with emergence-based group facilitation methods and who were eager to learn more.

Franziska Espinoza, manager for Culture Change at SwissCom IT Services, was an early participant at a seminar with Jim Rough in Germany. Finding this approach compatible with her existing practice, she pioneered the use of the Wisdom Council format (a large-group application of Dynamic Facilitation) within her company in Switzerland.

Manfred Hellrigl, director of the Büro für Zukunftsfragen (Department of Future-Related Issues) of Vorarlberg, Austria, also attended one of these early seminars. Manfred was on a quest for powerful and cost-effective public participation methodologies and quickly recognized the potential of Dynamic Facilitation in this regard. Between 2006 and 2012, the Büro sponsored more than twenty successful BürgerInnen-Räte (Citizen's Councils) in Austria using Jim's Wisdom Council model, and their work continues to grow and spread.

Each of these pioneers has contributed in multiple ways to the ongoing development and evolution of this work. Matthias zur Bonsen translated the 2008 version of the in-house manual into German and has written about his own discoveries while practicing and teaching this method. Franziska Espinoza created a six-minute video version of the Wisdom Council experience at SwissCom, with English-language subtitles, to help share this work more widely. She did this on her own time and initiative, as it lay beyond the scope of her organizational work. In 2012, Manfred Hellrigl and the Büro sponsored the first international gathering for Dynamic Facilitation practitioners, held in Vorarlberg, Austria.

All of these efforts, and those of many others, have contributed to the creation of a larger community of practice. In turn, our own practice evolves as we make new discoveries and share them with one another. Along these lines, I am especially indebted to the participants of the various workshops I have led: whenever I have the opportunity to teach, it deepens my own understanding of this work. For inviting me to teach and/or coordinating these workshops, a joyful thanks to Tom Atlee, Bronwyn Cooke, Lucy Lamkin, Ken Burrows, Sergio Lara, Brenda Thompson, Anne Erikson, Saul Eisen, Elmar Kruithoff, Manju Lyn Bazzell, John Abbe, Patrick Maxwell, Gina Cenciose, and Holger Scholtz. I also offer a deep bow and a heartfelt thanks to all of you who have attended as participants. While I am not listing you here by name, your energy and authentic engagement helped co-create our rich learning journeys together, and I am forever grateful.

Several key members of the Focusing community have appreciated the value of this work, recognized the parallels between the "outer listening" practice of DF and the "inner listening" practice of Focusing, and encouraged me in various ways to continue bridging these two worlds. My deepest thanks to Gene Gendlin and Mary Hendricks Gendlin, Joan Klagsbrun, Patricia Omidian, Nina Joy Lawrence, Ann Weiser Cornell, Jael Emberly, and Elmar Kruithoff.

There are a few other communities that I want to mention here. From 2001 to 2008, I participated actively on the IAF Group Facilitation listserv, impeccably moderated by Sandor Schuman. The participants on that list were notable for their intelligence, skillfulness, and generosity of spirit, and also came from a wide diversity of perspectives. This made for very rich collegial conversations that were a wonderful context in which to articulate my own experiences and develop my thinking.

From 2002 through the present, I have been an occasional participant on the ODNet listserv, generously moderated by Matt Minahan. This community, while very different in some ways, has also been a rich source of collegial fellowship, insight, provocation, and humor.

Last but not least, our small-but-growing online DF community has also been the source of rich support, encouragement, and learning, and I am very grateful to the various members who have posted there since we began in 2006.

Now that I am finally publishing the Dynamic Facilitation manual as a book, to make it available to a larger circle, I want to acknowledge

Lorna McLeod and John Eggen of Mission Publishing for their valuable support, my friend Ruth Hirsch for her insights and editorial feedback, and the highly talented and supportive people at Mill City Press for their assistance with this project.

I am also very grateful for the support of various mentors, coaches, cheerleaders, and friends along the way. In addition to those already mentioned above, Lyn Fine, Christine Kreminski, Angeles Arrien, Roger Harrison, Peggy Holman, Joe Shirley, and Tarra Christoff have offered invaluable encouragement and guidance at various points along the journey. Peggy Holman has also gifted me with her wonderful endorsement in the foreword to this book. Sandor Schuman and Gervase Bushe invited me to publish some of my earlier writings on Dynamic Facilitation and were extremely helpful with their incisive editorial wizardry. Raffi Aftandelian, John Falchi, Richard Moore, Alfred Rindlisbacher, and Veerle DeBock have all shown great enthusiasm for this work and have honored me with their generous friendship.

I am also very grateful to the many practitioners who have offered appreciative words and comments about the earlier versions of this manual. While I may not have kept track of all of your names, please know that the energy of your kindness is deeply inscribed in my heart and has helped sustain me along the sometimes arduous journey of midwifing an innovation.

The final word of thanks goes to you, dear reader. I welcome you to join our growing community of practice and look forward to hearing from you about your own experiences and insights!

REFERENCES

Bush, Robert A. Baruch, and Joseph P. Folger. *The Promise of Mediation: The Transformative Approach to Conflict*. San Francisco: Jossey-Bass, 1994.

Conklin, Jeffrey. *Dialogue Mapping: Building Shared Understanding of Wicked Problems*. Chichester: John Wiley and Sons, 2005.

Culmsee, Paul, and Kailash Awati. *The Heretic's Guide to Best Practices: The Reality of Managing Complex Problems in Organisations*. Bloomington, IN: iUniverse, 2011.

DeBono, Edward. *Serious Creativity: Using the Power of Lateral Thinking to Create New Ideas*. New York: HarperBusiness, 1992.

Holman, Peggy. *Engaging Emergence: Turning Upheaval into Opportunity*. San Francisco: Berrett-Koehler Publishers, 2010.

Holman, Peggy, Tom Devane, and Steven Cady. *The Change Handbook: The Definitive Resource on Today's Best Methods for Engaging Whole Systems*. San Francisco: Berrett-Koehler Publishers, 2007.

Owen, Harrison. *Open Space Technology.* Potomac, MD: Abbott
    Publishing, 1992.

Rogers, Carl. *Freedom to Learn for the 80s.* Columbus, OH: Charles E.
    Merrill Publishing Company, 1983.

Rough, Jim. *Society's Breakthrough: Releasing Essential Wisdom and Virtue
    in all the People.* 1stBooks Library. http://1stbooks.com, 2002.

Rough, Jim. "Using crises and teams to 'turn on' a system." *The Journal
    for Quality and Participation*, 25:1, 2002, 5–9.

Rough, Jim. "There's training and then there's Dynamic Facilitation and
    the magic of self-organizing change." *The Journal for Quality and
    Participation*, 20:3, 1997, 34–38

Rough, Jim. "Choice-creating: How to solve impossible problems." *The
    Journal for Quality and Participation,* 14:5, 1991, 54–59.

Zubizarreta, Rosa. "Practical dialogue: Emergent approaches for effective
    collaboration." In *Creating a Culture of Collaboration: The
    International Association of Facilitators Handbook*, ed. Sandor P.
    Schuman, 256–278. San Francisco: Jossey-Bass/Wiley, 2006.

Zubizarreta, Rosa. "Co-creative dialogue for meeting practical challenges:
    New approaches." *OD Practitioner,* 45:1, 2013, 47–53.

POSTSCRIPT

I hope you have found this manual useful. If you have any questions,
feedback, or stories about your own experiences with
Dynamic Facilitation, it would be great to hear from you.
You can reach me via e-mail at rosa@diapraxis.com.

If you would like support in learning the practice of
Dynamic Facilitation, I offer public workshops, customized in-house
trainings, coaching, and organizational consulting. Please contact
me through my Web site at www.DiaPraxis.com.

Jim and Jean Rough are the creators of this approach,
the originators of the term "Choice-Creating," and the founders of
Dynamic Facilitation Associates. For more information about their
seminars, please visit the DFA Web site at
www.DynamicFacilitation.com.

INDEX